HAIL,
AMERICAN
DEVELOPMENT

BY ELI SIEGEL

Hot Afternoons Have Been in Montana: Poems

*James and the Children: A Consideration of
Henry James's The Turn of the Screw*

The Aesthetic Method in Self-Conflict

Is Beauty the Making One of Opposites?

Art As Life

Psychiatry, Economics, Aesthetics

Shakespeare's Hamlet: Revisited

*Williams' Poetry Talked About by Eli Siegel and
William Carlos Williams Present & Talking: 1952*

HAIL,

AMERICAN

DEVELOPMENT

BY ELI SIEGEL

Definition Press · New York

Some of the poems in this volume were first printed in the following magazines: *Kauri, Today's Japan, The Literary Review, Definition, Prism International, Poor Old Tired Horse, Literary Review* of the *New York Evening Post, The North American Review;* in the International Graphic Arts Society catalogue; and as Terrain Gallery broadsides.

Standard Book Number 910492-10-7
Library of Congress Catalog Card Number 68-56296

Manufactured in the United States of America
by the Haddon Craftsmen.

CONTENTS

Contents

Contents

Contents

PREFACE

IF THE sameness and difference of America were to become musical, it would be poetry.

Every fact has music in it. The poet looks for it.

The visual, solid, historical structure of things in America looks for its or their music. Let us see that things in America get their music, the music which is themselves.

Every city, town, place in the United States is a study in history, crowded history, and aesthetics. The cities and towns of the United States have undergone the recent history of the land, a history not so representative of what America means.

America is difference and sameness trying to be seen as justice; and justice as warmth is love. Should the permanent in America be seen in the hours of a day, that would be a tremendous development.

Hail, American Development, a poem in *Hot Afternoons Have Been in Montana,* describes the America, I think, we want to begin with.

A city in southwestern United States has the everlasting in it, even while people walk in it. As I considered the matter, I found I was thinking of a city west of 100° longitude and north of 35° latitude. Liberal, Kansas could do very well. But other places in Kansas and places in Oklahoma and Texas would be right.

I take *Hail, American Development* from the book of 1957:

> There is that city,
> With white in its center,
> And white in its edges.
> Somewhere in the southwest,
> Across several creeks, several hills, several valleys,
> This city's to be got to.
> Seventy autumns this city's had,
> (Not counting this year).
> At any one moment in the afternoon
> Two women are walking south and north,

Two men north and east,
Two men west.
The river near it has been noticed.
And a warm boat is on it now;
Southwest, southwest of reposing tracks,
And houses near railroad stations.
Hail, American development.

The purpose of the poem was to juxtapose and mingle the aesthetic necessities, the aesthetic everlastingness of reality with people living their lives and being somewhere at any moment of the day. Meanwhile, in the neighborhood, geography was busy with visible and walkable-on constancies.

There is white in any city, town, place of Kansas, Oklahoma, Texas. The city has a center. The city has edges. There is white there. Reality and aesthetics are in white, and it is hard to tell reality and aesthetics apart in white.

And people are busy as we think of white as real and aesthetic —white is always a oneness of assertiveness and yieldingness, of intensity and hesitancy.

Creeks accompany people and white. Creeks, like white, are bold and modest. Hills are about. Hills are audacious compared to a plain—but hills as earth rising are modest. We can also find valleys near this southwestern place of the United States. At this moment we say in another way: Hail, American development.

Poetry is like white, a creek, a hill, a valley—a junction of boldness and modesty, a mysterious instantaneity of hard and soft.

And the city can be got to in many ways. A city is a center with surprising radii which are directions to and from it.

The southwestern city now developing can be thought of as having had seventy autumns. Of course, it has had more. It is right, however, to endow a place with seventy autumns and stay there.

Time and place are one as two women in an afternoon moment walk south and north. Moment, women, walking, south and north have been correctly liked by the Muses.

As two men walk north and east, and two men west, abstraction is embodied by men we may know. The embodying of abstraction is reality work and poetry work: also work of the visual arts. The abstraction of body is a work complementary to this work.

Southwest as such is a poetic idea. Think of what it is and see if you are not nearer to Keats' Nightingale or Lewis Carroll's Snark.

Warm boat and southwest are a couple worth knowing.

And there are houses and railroad stations.

It is an everlastingness and something now going on. Is it not well to say, Hail, American Development?

Is the seeing of Development as something which just is, in poetic territory? Keats' Grecian Urn poem intimates that when the moving, the bustling, the busy, the eager are seen as containing the timeless, poetry is furthered.

Hail, American Development!—because respect for the everlasting can help the daily and weekly. Moreover, using the utterly permanent as a means of being just to the possibilities of the week, is poetic and, as Percy Bysshe Shelley might say (see *A Defense of Poetry*), good politics, good legislation.

ELI SIEGEL

June 1968

HAIL,
AMERICAN
DEVELOPMENT

Litany of Presidents, Mostly Unfortunate

John Adams is our first unfortunate President, for people felt he
was too fussy and not wholly for their liberties and dignity;
and so he had only one term, which at that time was rather
humiliating.

But John Adams, while uncertain about sedition laws and France,
did not persist in ending the lives of many people he did not
know.

And Martin Van Buren is an unfortunate President with only one
term; a President seen as too smooth in politics and too much
given to seeing people as political possibilities.

But Martin Van Buren had no chance to be greatly unkind as our
contemporary President has been.

William Henry Harrison is unfortunate, for he died so soon, and
one can say that he was not considerate of Indians and thought
of them too much as living beings to be beaten—this was so
at Tippecanoe; and also he was an instrument of those who
saw him as a means to their power.

But William Henry Harrison did not put America into a new
position, frightening and low.

John Tyler was an accidental President and was ambiguous in his
one term;

But America even so looked good to other lands.

James Knox Polk made himself ridiculous by justifying a war with
Mexico we did not need and were not right in having;

But Polk listened to people, and people saw him soon as he was,
and so he was out of the Presidency before mischief was too
great.

Zachary Taylor was ineffectual, brief, and confusing; and Millard
Fillmore, another accidental President, did not write his
name deeply in American history.

Yet these did not make America look new and worse.

Franklin Pierce was impelled not so rightly, but there was a
dignity in the one term of this President.

James Buchanan chose wrongly, but what he did was in keeping
with what he had been in his easier days.

(Meanwhile it should be mentioned that we see George Washington, Thomas Jefferson, James Madison, James Monroe, and Andrew Jackson as fortunate Presidents.)

And we come now to the most fortunate President of all: fortunate in death.

Abraham Lincoln had America speak well of him in a time of uncertainty and pain.

There was something in Abraham Lincoln that saw what America hoped for.

He is a fortunate President.

Andrew Johnson is with the unfortunate; but his fussiness is likable and his quarrelsomeness does not reach degradation.

Ulysses S. Grant is not fortunate as President.

He simply should not have been.

America looked a little incongruous while he was President.

Yet it was recognizable, and true to earlier centuries.

Rutherford Birchard Hayes is unfortunate: he began without the serenity an election can mean.

Mighty he was not; he was decorous in absence of grandeur.

James Abram Garfield was unfortunate: a thoughtful person submerged by and using the political ways of the time.

He died unfortunately, clearly unfortunately.

Chester Alan Arthur as President cannot be called fortunate.

But there was an elegance he showed America could have, and there was the ethics that can be within a structure of acquisitive politics.

Grover Cleveland is fortunate narrowly—fortunate with his two terms.

Benjamin Harrison is unfortunate and recessive.

William McKinley is acutely unfortunate, standing for an America careless with the feelings of other lands; yet while he was President one could recognize America.

Theodore Roosevelt was fortunate because, with all his thinking from the top and disrelish of quiet, accurate, kind profundity, he set Americans to thinking of what they owed to each other.

And misfortune can be seen in William Howard Taft as President, for what people were was too distant from him.

Woodrow Wilson is unfortunate, for he made people hope in a way that his life belied.

Warren Gamaliel Harding is with the unfortunate, for he was not serious enough as to the meaning of America.

Misfortune also is exemplified by Calvin Coolidge, devoted to narrowness.

4

Among the unfortunate is Herbert Hoover, not able to relate a
   sense of the world to his own ambition, comfort, coldness,
   exclusiveness.
Among the fortunate is Franklin Delano Roosevelt, because there
   was an impulsion in him to find what people really hoped
   for: here he is like Queen Elizabeth.
The falsity of Harry Truman puts him with the unfortunate, and
   his unwillingness to see feeling in Asia makes him much
   like the great unfortunate now President.
With the unfortunate is the gobbling and shallow Dwight D.
   Eisenhower, after approval by the approved of.
John Fitzgerald Kennedy, with a mind caring and uncaring, not
   sure of what it loved, is with the unfortunate.
But the greatest unfortunate of all who have been President is
   Lyndon Baines Johnson, for it is in his Presidency that
   America looked so different.

And It Does, Marianne

O, in evening, Marianne,
With evening different everywhere,
Young men think of their past,
And think, too, of what the hell may be coming to them when
   coming days will have come to them, these thinking young
   men with a past and with desires.
Meanwhile, winds may be dying,
Or, somewhere, somewhere else, this is what it means for evenings
   to be different, winds may just be starting to be getting really
   strong,
And may now be sending paper on the street or in a road higher,
   almost or nearly, than paper ever went before, with winds
   doing the sending of paper to the sky.
(The sky just has to be, will be always, whether paper's going up
   or no.)
Coming to these young men, Marianne:
While in thousands of rooms under an early beginning moon,
   ties are being used to help along young men's necks in
   streets, and socks are being put on feet more or less rightly,
   being put on, anyway, usefully,
While thousands of young men think of the present and coming
   evening, and of other evenings and days,

5

O, Marianne, the sun is ready to come again,
And it will come, and how Marianne.
Without the sun, Marianne, ties would not be put on.
Without the sun, Marianne, socks wouldn't come to young men's
feet neatly, usefully.
Even, Marianne, without the sun winds would not be to do the
things winds do do and do.
It's a very connected world, Marianne.
Emptiness, just so, isn't had at all, Marianne.
Young men have to do with ever so many million things, Marianne.
Marianne, it's a very connected world.
That takes you in, Marianne.
It should, I think, too.
You deserve it and the world does.
So let be as is this universe.
Quite, Marianne.
Quite so, this universe, Marianne.
Marianne, as had this universe.
What do you say, girl?
It means something to me, what you say about this, girl.
You know it does.
And it does.
And it does, Marianne.

What Now Coheres—Of 1861-1865?

We're closer to the year, a hundred years
Ago, when war began, our Civil War.
As time goes on (or seems) our thoughts are more
Than ever, ever given to those fears,
Those rallyings, those yells, those skies. Appears
Again, the death at less than twenty-four
Of yelling Richard Tingley; with a store
Of other deaths. We ask: What now coheres—

Of all the gone, May 3rd, at Chancellorsville?
Atlanta's speeches, Hood's advance, retreat?
The length of Lincoln, lying known and still?
A picket's bellyache, a bullet neat;
The creeks with hissing shells; a mule named Bill;
The James in sunlight, and one's severed feet?

6

Necessity and Choice Always Prevail

He could have picked up
What he called the water-stopper
There in the white sink
Either by the little ring
Higher than the rest of the water-stopper;
Or by the round part in rubber,
Lower than the ring.
This he would do by
Applying thumb and third finger
Courageously, firmly and simultaneously
To the rubber in roundness of the water-stopper.
There is a choice about how to lift a water-stopper of this kind.
There is choice in the world.

II
However, if the ring has gone from the rubber of the water-stopper,
And you lift the water-stopper for some reason,
With ring gone—
You want to lift it perhaps, even, to throw it away,
There is no choice.
You have to lift it by the roundness in rubber.

III
Necessity then prevails.
Necessity and choice always prevail.

And There Are New Smiles; New Smiles

These were smiles, and now after the coming and going of many
    suns (the coming and going sun, always with us, always) new
    smiles are, and how new frowns, how new smiles; new people.
With the coming and going of suns, or a sun—one can be used—
    new smiles; new joys; new silences; new longings; new griefs;
    with the coming and going of a sun, new ideas.
O, there, a lady and a man, a way of saying a girl and a man, are
    smiling and frowning these days, and doing things smiling and
    frowning.
Where once other boys and girls were, other persons, other things
    were, now new smiles are

7

O, going of many suns; O, many reddenings of skies; O, otherness
    now; there, grief again, a world with us something like the
    world talked of once.
There, ladies and men, we have with us a newly smiling and
    frowning world, made up, much of it, of planning, feeling,
    paining, longing boys and girls.
Skies still redden.
Skies still wane.
And there are new smiles; new smiles.

Hell, What Is This About, Asked Again

When love a little came for the first time to James,
A growing boy,
Who had been all for roller-skates before, and matches between
    boys and boys with James among them,
James, like the not too knowing lad that he was, thought, in his
    heart, in his bones, in his flesh, thought, thought, thought,
    Hell, hell, what is all this.
Hell, hell, what is all this, he thought and love went on.
Bodies went on by him in the street, thoughts went on in him, in
    the street, and Hell, hell, thought James Rowan, what, what *is*
    all this, this about.
And then when Jane did her lovely, ugly, puzzling, deep, girl
    things, and James' bones, heart, flesh, mind, was all for Jane,
    for James, 'fore God, loved Jane—O, you big, great, great
    Jane,—James thought, cried, thought, moaned, bellowed,
    shouted, whispered, groaned, said, bellowed, Hell, hell, what
    is all this, this about.
Jane, that great thing, loved James a little, enough to pain James
    as much as nature, cruelty, the world wanted for the time.
James, you are having old pains, as old as the oldest stone the loving
    geologist finds; think, at times, of new roller-skates, but love,
    love is with you, and love is as old as, bigger than, the old,
    big, uncaring, hot sun.
James, see Jane, and shiver; James, think of Jane, and groan;
    James, imagine Jane, and sigh; it's all old stuff, and as big as
    any stuff there is.
Jane Terell, whatever she is, is as big as anything now; the girl's
    great, the girl's big, the girl's got tragedy with her.

8

Let her be pert, let her smile falsely, let her run gaily, falsely, the
     girl's great; it's coming to her that she take your bones, heart,
     soul, flesh, James.
Hooray for the inevitable, hooray for the immense—and James
     Rowan says, What the hell, hell, hell, is this, this about?
It is a good question.
James Rowan, 14, is great.
James Rowan, of Taunton, Massachusetts, on a nice, shady street,
     where there's good roller-skating, is infinite, is immense, is
     infinite.
It is a good question: Hell, what is *this* about.
It is a good question, friend, James Rowan.

A Hundred Plants on an Estate

You know there are a hundred
Plants on that estate; and some morning
When it is quiet, let us, you and I, Dora,
Go there and look at them.
You may, if it pleases you, touch the twenty-fifth
We notice; you may touch the fortieth.
The forty-first you may touch with your lips.
Such wonderful vegetation is on this estate.
If you stay long enough, you may
See the moon from a place on this estate.
You may, standing near one of the plants,
Distinguish a definite part of the somewhat lighted air.
You may hear sounds standing on this estate
At two o'clock in the afternoon; and at two o'clock at night
You may hear the wind moving trees and grass.
Indeed, this estate possesses
Such admirable natural belongings.
Imagine now: you can touch green on it,
Look at red,
Look at yellow.
Walking, you may view pink.
This pink estate is highly magnificent, surely.
Surmise any color,
And this estate, you may surmise, can have it.
Surmise any plant that Spain has
And this estate, you may conceive, can have its like.

This estate has noble European parallels.
It is envied by magnifico after magnifico.
It is a glorious possession, set amidst boiling ocean.
It is the frenzied, comely point of a furious, godlike process.
It is night's dearest content, to which it is like a strawberry to a
    strawberry,
One green leaf to one green leaf.
It is infinitely commendable, and it is, Harold,
Luscious, luscious, luscious; luscious, as berries suffused by
    ethereal cream,
Suds softened by the interposition of unerring divinities.
This estate is English,
And when English moons, English tongues, English words
Are about,
Then, Harold and Dora,
It is at its boilingest,
Its most immensely proud,
This to be visited, visited,
Lying softly, daringly, abidingly,
Possessed estate,
Which we shall visit
Tomorrow, after careful preparing.

And There Prevail

Brooklyn the gorgeous,
The southern Nineveh,
Where once on fields near an ocean not to be named now, prowlers,
    aborigines (Mr. Peckham) went about; and later not one of
    these got into learned books many of them now in Brooklyn
    by the Sound.
How few, few persons, prowling or others, get, feet, spirit and all,
    into books; take the form, they, these feeling objects, of print
    now neatly reposing in the learned hush of cities.
Dissoluteness is in Brooklyn and how few, few depraved people
    are remembered.
Brooklyn has all of Nineveh's sins, otherwise in the disposition by
    existence of sins and sin-having powers, there would be a
    Frightful, Cavernous, not-to-be dreamed of thing in logic
    (Miss Welsham perhaps talking).

10

It was logic Asshur-bani-pal used in the smiting and smiting of his
    Oriental foes, and the putting to great, various pains of his
    smitten, living foes.
Beings in Brooklyn have thought of Nineveh, and seemingly in a
    fashion, Nineveh knows not of Brooklyn.
Brooklyn doesn't know everything in altogether free depravity and
    knavery, but no place near or far from ocean does.
How is it that of a hushed afternoon a man may drowse in
    Brooklyn with his elbow near the name Palmyra.
It may be that Nineveh is talked of by a person with his mouth
    somewhat full of some vegetation favored by tall, river-
    running-about American aborigines.
Brooklyn, dear, you rest somewhere around anonymous Assyrians
    and could-be-named American-born Indians.
I say you are gorgeous; your temples magnificently send their
    sleepily terrifying smoke to Eastern skies.
Though trolleys reach you with mothers who know hatpins,
    family-bibles and America of some years ago, you are no less
    Nineveh than Nineveh is.
I could say Nineveh is in those family-bibles had by much-weighing
    ladies who have curves and straight lines and curves rather
    far apart.
Fatness, O Brooklyn, is just as much Assyrian, just as much
    Eastern, of the East with chariots and wide swords.
I can imagine aged goers-about in Nineveh, drowsing, looking at
    something, becoming confused, and thinking of something
    nearer Brooklyn than Orenotep is.
Burnish, O Brooklyn, the chariots of iron that have horses go
    before them off to battle having much iron.
Flash, Brooklyn, with all your Eastern towers by the Sound.
Have, Brooklyn, the pains of not-daringness the way Nineveh has.
Mist, Brooklyn, comes to sin, and soils and embellishes your
    many-windowed, exotic edifices.
Allar-hata-pan, great, cruel man of war, is a Brooklyn man, though
    not born there.
Fidget at peace, Brooklyn, and wish for times when spears go
    deeply into the cunning withinnesses of beings.
Eighty thousand voices, well-timed, say, greatly, Brooklyn is
    gorgeous.
Gorgeous and sad, O Nineveh.
Gorgeous and many, O Nineveh.

Dissolution's in thee, Brooklyn, and the ocean and streams by you
    run with the blood of the slain and sick.
Hours are everything.
Boom, O chariots,
And to Brooklyn go
And there prevail.

On American Boys Dying in 1863, in Virginia, and Later Elsewhere

The uniform is gray
Of bodies lying still.
The battle of that day
Is Chancellorsville.

Americans lie dead
An evening of May.
It hasn't yet been said
They all were right that day.

Musings on Distinguishing an Israeli Cellist from Other People in a World Like This

So many people are not Israeli cellists.
Nevertheless, you could not distinguish an Israeli cellist
From a number of people
Quietly walking down Park Avenue South.
The only time you can be sure you are looking at an Israeli cellist
Is when you are at a concert having one,
And there is an announcement telling clearly
That a certain person
Is an Israeli cellist
And not something else.
Should this take place,
You can be rather sure.
Otherwise, the best thing to do
Is to presume that there are Israeli cellists
And wait for the moment
Of certainty, clearness, nothing but that.

Aurungzebe

Aurungzebe, he
Was a baby;
Mahomet
Was seen to fret;
Napoleon
From the cradle's gone;
Cromwell,
Some tell,
A froward infant
Was the instant
He came to
The world he knew
Later as
Protector of England; has
A crocodile not
Its beginning days? and in a cot
That villain was;
And what does
Primitiveness mean,
If in it is not seen
Weeness, babyness
Of nations, generals, plants,
Houses, wires, aunts?

Consider Now

Consider now the sun of day;
And the moon that comes at night;
What's in them, and what's the way
The cause of both shows its might

In them; and what may be between
Them, as two things of one kind,
Working together as may be seen.
—And we must keep the earth in mind.

O, Wounded Birds

Maybe it was not the sound
Of the battle of Pavia as then
It could be heard; at least it was the sound
Of America's leaves, October,
Rustling in the breeze,
By the still Ohio.
O, maybe it was not the cry
Of a bird wounded when
The battle of Pavia was at its fiercest.
But I know it was the sound
Of a bird joyously singing
When the sun was bright
After two days of rain,
And something more than two.
O, wounded birds, despair not
Of seeing bright suns again
After days of rain.
Sounds are of every second,
And seconds come again, again.
O, sweet wounded bird,
You yet will have rain again,
And sun and rain and sun.

Zeb Duryea

What, in our orange world,
Is like Zeb Duryea,
Woodcutter and moon-watcher?
He has seen thousands of wings,
And, thousands of times, smoke from pipes rising.

Leaves Stick on the Coat Collar

Leaves that fly against the face,
And stick on the coat collar are children of the lovely Diana.

There Is That in You Which Won't Be Fooled, Johnson; And It Is Liked by the World

There is some opinion one has of oneself,
However little known it is.
What one sees as to oneself may, sadly, be far off,
And not a part of afternoon doings.
Even so, this opinion of ourselves
Cannot be fooled,
For it is the same as the world's opinion of ourselves,
The world of all time, of anywhere, of any moment, any possibility.

II
As we go to bed, the world goes with us,
And is in us, considering.
It is the world as ourselves that goes with us to sleep of a night,
And lies with us on a pillow;
And may make us frown,
Without our seeing a frown;
And may make us sigh,
Without our knowing anything about a sigh.

III
Whatever it is,
Whatever you name it:
Conscience or the world in us as ourselves,
The still small voice or Sweat,
God or outraged public opinion—
Whatever, whatever you name it,
It can't be fooled,
For it is the world;
And the world, though changeable,
And relative and all and all,
Is what it is—nevertheless—
And won't be fooled,
And can't be.

IV
There is something of the world in you, Johnson,
Which can't be fooled.
The world hovers about a President's brow
As much as about any brow.
The world gets under a President's eyelids

15

As much as under any eyelids whatsoever.
And the world is present in the intricate withinness
Of a President with weight;
And in the intricate withinness often accompanying life.
This intricate withinness
Has poetic corporeality
And somatic immeasurability
Even while it
Is included in an armchair.

v

Conscience and the somatic are friends.
Conscience and politics are friends.
Conscience and a Texas county are friends.
Conscience and a Minnesota township are friends.

VI

What is it, Oh Johnson, you are trying to fool, though you may
    not know it?
It is conscience saying:
Thousands of people in Asia are not enemies of Americans living
    between San Diego and Portland, Maine.
Thousands of people are not evil that much they should be aimed
    at by American machines.
What people in Vietnam are after is not so much against the
    Constitution and the Book of Common Prayer
They should become casualties announced in newspapers.

VII

There has to be good reason for the killing of anybody.
A good reason has to exist for the giving of anyone pain.
Do you care enough for the death of a person, the pain a person
    gets, a person with a corporeal withinness like yours?
Let's quit the grandiose as politics and international, symmetrical
    statement.
—Are people now dying who shouldn't,
And have not done evil,
And may be, even, in their way, on the side of good?

VIII

This is where you are trying to fool yourself, Johnson.
There is something in you that knows people are dying who don't
    have to.
The religion you are a member of doesn't go with this.

16

Alexander Campbell, who founded your particular mode of
worship, would not have stood for it.
He argued with other Christians, with other Protestants, with
Atheists, Deists, and so on,
But he would not have them die,
Or be in any way the cause of their dying.
Perhaps, after they died—these opponents—God would not deal
with them sweetly,
But that would be after their lives here.
Their lives could go on, and would not be stopped by Campbell's
strength.
And Alexander Campbell wrote a treatise called *Remission of Sin.*
That concerns you, President, occupier of so much space in bed
and no more.

IX

Take Alexander Campbell as a guide,
Rather than Moyers, Rusk, Stennis, McNamara, Lodge, Taylor,
Nixon.
They have the same trouble you have.
Their conscience—as the world in themselves—is too far off in
them, too disdained, too faint, too frail.
Listen to one Vietnam boy of 18, as you once listened to a Texas
boy of 18,
And listen better.
Because you are angry that you are not pleased enough with your
life,
Even as you are wealthy, financially ever so select, fiscally lofty,
Politically chosen for continental distinction and might,
National uniqueness—
Just because, with all this, you don't feel so at ease deeply—
Is no reason bodies should become still in jungles,
Arms should leave their bodies,
Napalm should take skin off bodies, and have bodies change to a
burned congeries and scorched welter,
Growing things should be changed into brown,
And bodies sent hither and thither by strategic bombing.

X

There is something in you that won't be fooled, Johnson.
It used to be called the still small voice—can be called that now.
The still small voice is also voices you know about in streets.
Manila has joined these voices.
This voice with many voices has been heard in West Berlin.

17

It has been heard in places with many books in California.
You can hear it in Quebec.
From ground in New Zealand it has risen.
God, how frequent it is in New York.
Your ugly counselor and servant, called technically Vice-President,
    has heard it in Australia.

XI

Hear, Oh Johnson, Oh President!—
There, under your chin,
Is a demonstration in you;
There is a picketing in you,
There is a clamor in you,
There is a criticism of your foreign policy in your very being,
There is the world's silent, constant walk-around.
Tell this, exuberantly, to Rusk, McNamara, Lodge.
It will help them.
There is a demonstration in you as on the streets of a capital in
    Europe, or Africa, or Asia, or Wisconsin.
The world's silent, constant walk-around is good also for Rusk,
    McNamara, Lodge.
Tell them of it as if it were a victory, fine for them also.
For it is that.
This demonstration—how wonderful—is the same
As that which won't be fooled in you, Johnson.

XII

Resuming (with a thought of Lookout Mountain, 1863, now in
    geographical wisdom):
There is that which won't be fooled in you, Johnson.
It is lovely and immortal.
It is liked by the world.

Only One Thing

How are we going to get the safe into the banana boat?
How are we going to get the adding-machine into the shrimp-boat?
This was the plaintive cry
That emerged from the delicate throat
Which had been used to scold only one thing so far:
DESTINY.

18

Those Green Dogs

Those green dogs which tumbled among
Warm flowers in late August
Were touched by the conservatively-clothed adult;
An adult who, in the house he lived in,
Was the only person who had read
The Livid Stain, a Scottish novel;
And one of the two who had seen
Hell's Raising, a movie.
Green dogs could scamper over three score copies of The Livid
     Stain
Or bark for many hours while Hell's Raising was being seen.
Lightly, let us go to the tombs of novel-readers
And over earth green dogs are in.
And flowers continue,
And are warm somewhere always
And droop in moonlight of many states.
And droop
While ocean's husky and well-disposed roar
Is heard in Scotland,
Or abroad.

Collins and Heroes

So the stars rested
As the little boy mused,
At five o'clock in the garden;
And clocks tolled heavily
Round many gardens
In the heavy November.
Thrushes were gone,
Grass had gone,
Green had gone.
There was a still of ages in the hall.
The boy's step was like a heavy gong, from a long time since.
The stars rested.
There were thuds after wars.
There were pictures after pictures.
There were smiles after thuds.
All was Collins and heroes.

Beginning with Footfalls about the Northern Dispensary, Greenwich Village: Summer, 2 A.M.

Sickness is that which brings together the avant-garde and the
ancient.

In the midst of Greenwich Village is a triangular building—so I
have seen it—which is called the Northern Dispensary;

And is at Christopher Street and Waverly Place, now, as it was in
the administration of Andrew Jackson and the mayoralty of
Walter Bowne.

Sickness, you will grant, is concerned with the eminent Andrew
Jackson and the not so eminent Walter Bowne.

Well, there were ailments among the people of New York,

And they came here—for it was a Dispensary—lovely word—

And something was done for them, and they didn't pay anything,
or paid little.

Sickness, we know, is concerned with money—as it is concerned
with a famous President and a distinguished Mayor.

From 1831 to 1840, from 1840 to 1850, from 1850 to 1860, and
then—right through the Civil War, persons whose names we
do not know came—and at what hours!—to this building, in
its architectural strangeness, and felt, each in their way,
something or other as they came home.

Ailments are so entwined with, run so deeply and variously
through all lives.

There is an engraving of the Northern Dispensary in Valentine's
Manual of the Corporation of the City of New York for 1859.

The engraving is so still.

There are a lamppost, trees, a lady and child and the skirt of the
lady is wide.

Two gentlemen converse under the Dispensary tree: the tree is
within a fence.

There is a wide, bold sign across the building, reading Northern
Dispensary, as if the city were proud.

And it is the building now with us, with the grand St. Vincent's
not so far away; and electronics employed to combat sickness,
and employed as entertainment.

The form of the Northern Dispensary says, with its strong angles,
ailments can be given conquering, everlasting symmetry.

See the form of the Northern Dispensary of—is it?—1827, and be
somewhat surer that disease is not the main thing, and can
be subjected to shape as power.

II

All the woes, vexations, little triumphs, perhaps big ones close to
 this Northern Dispensary, now visible!
An ailment makes man's mind a little different, and if you have
 to go to a Dispensary about that ailment, you feel something
 which should be known as a part of man's recorded wholeness.
A Dispensary like a church, a court, a ship, a library, a prison, a
 brothel, is a place where man's passion, man's littleness,
 divine fidgetiness can show themselves as explanatory of the
 balky nature of things.
Mornings in the Northern Dispensary in 1862—with relatives of
 New York dwellers at war in Virginia—these mornings can
 be in one's mind with mobile, strange usefulness.

III

I remember footfalls in a summer night, 2 A.M., some years ago
 about the Northern Dispensary.
They were Waverly Place footfalls and Christopher Street footfalls.
They said something of summer and deep night, of history and
 sickness, and the angular stolidity of a building which
 dispensed, with a municipality smiling, human requirements
 for human needs.
All in a late June night, after 2 A.M., there was thought like this,
Which, a short while ago repeated itself.
The building, the building is present.

IV

There is a list of "attending physicians" of the Northern Dispensary
 in the 1859 Valentine Corporation Manual of New York City
 I have mentioned.
J.W. Purdy, M.D., and S.B.W. McLeod, M.D., were the physicians
 whose assignment it was to combat, alleviate, understand
 "Women and Nervous Diseases."
E. Denison, M.D., and E.J. Hoffman, M.D., were meant to do good
 about Diseases of Children.
Consequently, Women, Nervous Diseases, Diseases of Children are
 together in real New York, American, Greenwich Village
 History.
What a challenge!—Women, Nervous Diseases, Diseases of
 Children!
Apollo, to the combat!

21

v

When I thought of the Northern Dispensary last, as architecture
and history,
I saw it as a sharp, quiet answerer—if it is given personality—
To much enveloping man sadly,
To much within man vexingly—
To people asking, furiously, What and Why?—in 1827; who have
never stopped, for others have taken their places.

Cooperating Meadows

The Confederate Generals
Roved the meadows,
At last understanding their error,
Seeing the ugliness of something,
Not calling something correct.
Ah, happy Confederate Generals,
At last seeing yourselves as scalawags,
As incomplete,
On the cooperating meadows.

Noise Is of All, The World

It all is noise.
When leaves fall, it is noise, and when love makes crying, sobbing,
sighing (these three) it is noise.
It is well known wars have noise all through them, of cannon, of
men, of trees shot down, falling by cannons' doing.
When wit is elegant, deep, wide, taking in much, and going deep
into the world (how deep the world can be gone into) it is
noise when it is said; it is noise.
When love is at its quietest and intensest, when sharp whispers are
the thing, maybe with dry branches shaking moodily, sharply,
outside, it all is noise.
Noise comes many ways.
It is sound.
It is of all, the world.
Noise is of all, the world.

22

A First in Music

Sometimes, what is near has to be seen as if it were not near.

Today, in my own home, Martha Baird told of how the Opposites, Sameness and Change were one in music; and how the opposites other than Sameness and Change were one in music, one in ourselves—if we see it—and one in the whole world of every minute, every happening, every distress.

It was in my own home, this showing; and I married her who spoke—but all time was present, and, I believe, what is to be.

The talk was not everything: there was scraggliness, faltering, uncertainty; but music was shown to be the structure of the world, was shown to be our desire, was shown to be with all the arts as a description, a replica, a containing of the world as strife and repose, horror and the bearable, the splintering and the one, the hideous and the absolute.

Benny Goodman was used: and Gene Krupa was used: and they were ready.

Antonio Vivaldi, and his sound, showed might and gentleness, difference and sameness—the unexpected and the inevitable as one.

Resurrected, glorious, buoyant, everywhere Antonio Vivaldi of now; and once, more confinedly, of the eighteenth century!

The graceful, exploring, transitional Wolfgang Amadeus Mozart of the bounding, sidestepping, falling, curving, insisting, reversing, proceeding Linz Symphony, was used by Miss Baird, all for a musical first.

Mozart is the opposites seen Mozartianly.

And Beethoven: there was stealthy, uncertain, level quiet changing on its own power, as itself, to a rise and a crash with sharply ascending, wide, uproarious confidence—what was in quietness and apprehension, changed while itself into transmuting crash.

Baird said, It was the opposites.

It was a first in music.

For Baird said it was the opposites:

Not hintingly, implicitly, uncertainly—but straightforwardly and forever.

Music rejoiced with a new, assertive clearness.

It is a beginning.

There was a drinking song of Beethoven,

Sung with a loud, clear guttural, in redolent, profound German by a singer of these days.

The opposites were in the Wein, Wein, Wein.

The opposites were in the trumpet,
The opposites were in the drums.
The opposites were in the Emperor Concerto managed deftly,
  circuitously, and loudly by Ludwig Van.
Vivaldi instanced the opposites in the Italy pre-American
  Revolution.
God, what a junction: astute helter-skelterness!
Martha Baird, yours is a first.
Others may not say so, but Music feels clearer, with today, August
  20, 1964.
There is no reason why this should not be so.
What, after all, were the world, Vivaldi, Bach, Mozart, Beethoven
  (otherwise Ludwig Van), Handel, Monteverdi, and yesterday's
  thrush and cataract working for?
You have told the central thing.
Music is clearer.
Music is more.
Music is more of our lives, more assertively, kindly of our lives.

Candor Will Be Mine

We aim to please the ladies that wander down these balustrades.
  Careful also of the satisfaction of the balustrades are we. We
  know that merry-go-rounds come to an afflicted earth, and
  not for many earths would we afflict merry-go-rounds.—When,
  candidly, one tells us he doesn't like balustrades, we just as
  candidly, and more quickly, tell him he does. For it is only
  polite to do this. Candor is just one of an innumerable group
  of virtues, and the groups are innumerable. Novels are
  written to aid candor. Ladies walk down balustrades to aid
  candor. And what are knees for?—to aid candor. The parallel
  construction is more than inevitably contingent on the
  circumstances. When merry-go-rounds come to balustrades,
  and all ladies are candid; and the haze that exists slowly of
  mornings candidly accompanies our candid eyes; and hearts
  are candidly gay; and all adverbs are candid and all adjectives
  are; and when revolutions occur because candor is lacking;
  and research is candid; and hey, all heys are; and huzzas—
Oh, me, candor will be mine.

Approaches

In Autumn
One leaf
Approaches
Another leaf.

All, All to Be Seen

Blustering Ted
Is now dead.
Impossible Susan
Died then.
Corrupt Alexis
After paralysis
Is dead, too.
People we'd boo
(And rightly)
After lives unsightly
Are in graves.
The way death behaves
Is worthy of
Commendation, love.
Blustering Ted
Has another chance.
Unendurable Fred
May advance.
Impossible Susan
May do better in
Another time and place.
Sneaky Grace
May be renewed,
As may Gertrude—
Lying and mean.
How death may bring
Better happening
To lives once lived:
And, perhaps, to be lived
Again; again:
All, all to be seen.

Boats, Shores, Tides, Fish

The Quadruple Wriggling Quality of Boats, Shores, Tides, Fish

Boats bump, graze shores
As tides flow toward shores
And fish don't mind.
But I mind,
Because unless you mind
There is no poem.

II

Boats can be rowed into unutterable distance
As you can.
Shores stay,
And that is something you want to do.
Tides show constancy
And you would like to have constancy.
Fish wriggle, and you do.

III

Boats, shores, tides, fish, wriggle into each other.
It is sort of pleasant,
Sort of necessary.

Become U-Nity

Boats, shores, fish, tides
Wrig-
Gle
Into each other, and look,
Become
U-
Nity.

The Theme Wriggles

As you look at a theme,
The theme wriggles,
As your mind does.
This happens with the theme,
Boats, Shores, Tides, Fish.
Maybe that's good.

Bulldog's Hair

For the musings were much,
And the apples were green,
There in a morning of attitudes and grimness,
There in a spot of wideness and flight.
Apples come to the touch,
To a furbelow, serene,
In an era of primness,
An era of sight—
As, Janet counted
In an anecdotal age
Of flightiness, guardianship, near to each other,
Beyond the breakers there
Where a major dismounted—
As is to be seen in a blurred page
Of a book, with which one could smother
An insect on a bulldog's hair.

This Spring, See the Forgiveness of Asian Flowers

That the flowers will keep on growing this Spring in America—
And it seems they will—
Shows that flowers are the most forgiving things in the growing
    kingdom—
Which includes so much.
There! the leaders of America
Kill in Asia—a wonderful place for flowers—
And flowers, living, will grow here too as if there was nothing to
    notice.
The kinship of American flowers with Asian flowers
Is one of the longest, truest, deepest, lovingest
Havings-to-do-with of things like each other, but in a different
    place.
—Wonder of wonder, the Asian flowers—there are many elsewhere
    than where American leaders killed and kept on doing this—
These Asian flowers
Feel it is all right for American flowers to grow this Spring.
This Spring, then,
We shall see American flowers grow;
And the forgiveness of Asian flowers.

27

Haikus: Some Instances

Haiku of Retraction

I said this myself.
I heard it again from Him.
I never said it.

The Sunflower's in League

A sunflower there
Is in league with cool, brisk brook
To which the sun comes.

You Can Watch

Sunflower begins.
Sometimes, a while, you can watch.
It, yourself, begins.

The Transforming Best

She liked that thing best.
What company it has, though!
Watch the best transform!

Seen

Apple, tomato
Walked down the fat road, redly,
In round friendship, Oh!

Invitation and Hope

Come see me, she said.
Yes, I don't want to be seen.
See what *you* can do.

Honor

Whirling banana
High over green, lasting earth:
Yellow is honor.

The Print

Can dark and light
Show wrong and right?
—And round and straight
Show love and hate?
—And dim and clear
Show hope and fear?

The Song of the Potter: Ceylon Folk Poem

My fine pots,
My beautiful plates,
Made of the good earth of Kélany.

My beautiful plates,
My fine pots,
Heated in the sun and polished well.

Into huts and palaces,
Pots and plates, go, go;
Carry to the famished
Sinners or saints
The most beautiful and the largest grains.
Pour, so that they be not thirsty,
To the elect and to the damned,
The divine draught of earth.

Do not give
To the sick nor to the weary
Bad plants, vile herbs;
But, sure friends,
Give them, as healing,
Good roots and honest herbs.

My fine pots,
My beautiful plates,
Made of the good earth of Kélany.

Chapped Second Fingers

In the midst of January
It is good to think of cherry-
Blossom time, some months away.
January has been relentless—that is,
Cold; and we know it can be.
It should, then, enable us to prize the ripple
In warmth, the green in fresh, restrained heat.
January must be useful
Towards making us see the red of summer,
Of cherries, for instance—and at noon
There are lanes with thick leaves above them,
Hanging properly from branches, on branches,
In June summeriness, July wide hotness.
All this is meant to insult
Unkempt and nipping January,
Brutal month, of ice, and winds from rivers (to the west),
Of sleighs perhaps, and chapped second fingers.

Character Sketch

I am no good.
No one knows it as well as I do.
Even the world I came into is not so good.
But I haven't done with it as well as I could.
When I talk, people are not improved.
When I talk, people are often less cheerful.
When people talk, I am often less cheerful.
When I succeed, it is on a matter which doesn't make much
    difference whether I succeed or fail.
I don't know how to insult people: my best insults are under my
    breath.
I get ordinary ailments.
I think of being distinguished, but I get afraid.
I am a scatterbrain.
Even on the subject of why I am no good, it seems I am a
    scatterbrain.
Having too much good will, and for too many people, scares me
    completely

I am foolish in unknown ways.
My mistakes are monotonous.
I can be bored at the drop of a hat,
And I can bore a person at the drop of a glove.
Poetry has no steady friend in me.
The Renaissance is so far off, it seems like dim water.
I don't know whom I'm talking to, so I talk.
I am a hodge-podge,
And I feel safe because I am a hodge-podge,
But so dissatisfied—
And also so lazy, and so afraid.

Milwaukee Eagle

O Milwaukee eagle, circler over muddy rivers,
Who takes the sun contentedly and air approvingly;
Who never has alighted on languidly carried parasols had by tall
    ladies in brown;
Who has seen sheet-iron all the while preferring clouds—
You can be the life's-soothing of Miss Halloran, of John Doonane.
Cross long tracks, clean in your sun, eagle, and wheel over 400
    rosebushes, many, many white.
You take your sky-nearing head to cities possessing the tired at 9
    and the moody at 11.
You possessed the moment's notice of the much and dimly in love
    Al Hamber, who also is around a machine which has written
    the number 14, and the number 4.
Something like a rhombus is made by your busy this way, that
    way wings, in the gently embracing sky, having you.
You are not a civic problem to Milwaukee.
You do not irk Milwaukee householders, given to dozing when the
    sun is red.
You do not question time and what air is and space is is not matter
    of annoyance to you.
Milwaukee eagle, impoliteness is not for you, not in you, any way
    at all.
Take your mornings blithely, much flying one.
Be worthy of the sun, you, at home where all is high.
Disregard all two-legged, no-winged sojourners.

Traverse the sluggish creek, the buoyant brook, the unconcerned
   river.
Be unaware of any star but in that manner you choose.
Take dark gracefully, light becomingly.
Adorn mist and add to the power of rain.
Beyond snow, be gravely still and pleased.
Take Milwaukee as you please.
You have your rights, eagle, and your mad privileges, your not to
   be ever taken away bird and being madnesses.
Skirt against light and charge white air, reposing clouds; do this,
   and, eagle, the world is pleased and says, Go on.
You go over Milwaukee, but Milwaukee is your debtor.
Be seen when you may.
See hats 2000 feet down.
Sleep in clouds.
Be over Milwaukee.
Get into dreams.
Milwaukee eagle, be mad and rest; be seen and untroubled;
       surround houses and be the despair of gentlemen, the favorite
       of air, the pampered of earth, and the swift decoration of
       Milwaukee and furious, strange, unthought of, wide heights,
       yours, O eagle.

1967: The American Past Will Come Later

Was ever country more a thing of shame
Than ours, the country of the many bombs?—
With cheapness that which more and more becomes
The centre of the mind in those who claim
To represent us? How our land seems tame
With ugliness it has, for something numbs
The most of us: our ethics have no drums.
There is a simmer where there should be flame.

But flame will be! How cleansing it will be!
It will ennoble cheapness; change the grime.
The flame, America, will beat the slime
Our carelessness has fostered. Gods! we'll see
A land as kind as rivers are, as high
As mountains are.—The past, the land, are why.

Ode on the Death of a Racketeer

Exactly what is racketeering,
That puts a man in a hospital with his chest plugged,
And his insides streaming?
It is what college economists call the free market,
Smugly of a college morning—
Competition unspoiled by public law.
Schultz was a hero of laissez-faire.
His death is a blow to individual enterprise.
Hail Schultz, O college wise men,
Who died for the cause you talk about.

The Siamese Tell Us: Let Us Listen

The Siamese cats in our building,
And we are blessed with quite a few,
Have been uttering their sad, hoarse cry
More than is customary
In the last days.
And we pondered:
What is their message?
And the only conclusion we could come to
That had depth and coherence
Was that these pussycats, after all,
Were once of Siam,
These years called Thailand.
And they know
In their primeval fashion
That the American army
Intends bad things for Siam or Thailand:
Bases in which to awe and put down
Asian stirrings for the governments they care for.
And so our Siamese pussycats,
Enlisted by their very nature
In the cause of justice
And the old true cause of humanity and America,
Are now saying they see what is going on.
God bless complaining Siamese,
And may their message effectively reach
All the States of this tormented Union.

Rain in Ireland

Rain in Ireland, once,
With England near,
Rain over soft, green meadows in Ireland.
And England was near,
The Atlantic was near.
Monks were in Ireland then;
And in black monasteries, listened to the rain, and saw it falling,
    falling on soft, green, green fields in Ireland.
A girl far off was going fast to her home, a low hut, low and black,
    now in rain.
England was near.
London was near.
The Atlantic was near.

Picketing God, Or Something to Be God

We are picketing God.
We are demanding that our lives make sense.
We are demanding that our lives have something to do with
    everything we meet and with all time.
We want a sense of forever.
We are against narrowness and temporariness.
We demand that death fall into place honestly and agreeably.
We do not wish to be foaming fractions.
We are tired of seeming bubbles (bubbles swiftly vanishing into
    blah indignity).
We are against disguises that disgust with the years.
We wish this moment to stand, somehow, always.
We shout against degrading and sickening impermanence.
We wish to be wretches with radiance, if wretches we have to be.
We want clearness that has aroma in the world, warm and
    authentic, and withstanding all looking at.
We are picketing God.

And if God isn't here to be picketed, why then we picket
    What Is,
And say it must be God.

Poem about an Ancient Instrument

If you put
An ancient instrument
In wild grass,
It'll stay there.

The Little Cube in Space

Somewhere in space
A cube of air
When thought of is
Quite debonair.

The little cube
Is not, unless
It has our thought
And friendliness.

Red and Yellow and Hills

Often, you know, when trains in autumn,
Pass near hills full of dead leaves, gone long from trees,
The trains move the leaves, and winds help the trains.
By hills in autumn, in smoky autumn, smoking trains go,
Fast; and leaves drift listlessly down hills near speedy, dashing
trains.
The hills are red and yellow; and the speedy, dashing train is
black; and white smoke comes from the train; and the train
whistles wildly, piercingly, and leaves, dead, autumn leaves drift
listlessly down old hills.
Cry, train, cry, leaves, cry, hills.
Train, dash wildly.
Leaves, die.
Autumn's here and the hills are.
Autumn's here, and haze and smoke in sky, and sultrily, faintly red
sun goings-down in autumn.
Smoke's in the sky, quietly, lazily.
Trains and trains go by, whistling wildly, piercingly.
Dead leaves drift along lazily.
Autumn's here and quiet, and red and yellow and hills.

Invective Against Lake Superior

How from the honeycomb of time
Come shoes and stones and you,
Sitting there indifferent,
Not thinking of Charles V at all,
Hapsburg emperor of once.
It is enough to make one want to throw
Square tons of marble into Lake Superior,
Which now seems also indifferent.
Such a lake!
The honeycomb of time had better go about its business
Some other way
And make that lake seem springy and aware.

Point

This is now sad brown earth which once had pink waving on it and
    long pink waving by merry water.
In this earth are the prints of hundreds of persons, hand in hand,
    walking—seeing the eyes of one dearer than any eyes and the
    hand of one more joyous than any hand; here on this sad earth
    have these persons' greatest feeling gone along.
Feeling is possessed by sad, brown earth going on now to one of its
    many winters when white will be where pink and yellow were.
Hand in hand, walking, have persons gone across yellow and pink
    and green; shoulders meeting, the dearest shoulders there were.
To merry water have shoulders gone, around and over pink and
    red, yellow, and over the sad brown of once.
This point has had the triumphant Margaret; the very pleased
    Constantia; the not for the while moody Alice; it has had the
    raging Arthur and the gay Edward; the victorious William;
    somewhere in this sad earth is the print of Arthur's white foot
    and Elvira's slippered one.
Flowers and grass were noticed by Fred and Anita going over green
    to merry, moving water.
Sad earth, having yellow and red falling to you where once, in
    August and in May, stepped the beaming Ethel and the rapt
    Ermengarde.
Sad earth, possessing 400 Margarets, 400 Jims.

Gaze

Gaze, O traveller
On old pines.
Let the pines meet your eyes.
Be tearful looking at old pines.

Running Oxen

O, wielder of many hoofs,
You can break many heads,
And kill many boars,
And put inside of running oxen the piercing steel, the quickly
   entering iron.

Condign Punishment for Our Leader

On December 7, 1967, Our Leader took part in the funeral services
   for Cardinal Spellman.
From this comes the idea of a just punishment for Our Leader, the
   cause present in so many deaths in Asia.
This punishment would be Lyndon Baines Johnson attending the
   funeral of every person killed needlessly in Vietnam.
Our Leader would look at the dead body of a boy of eight, and,
   conspicuously, be of the funeral.
The next day he would attend the funeral of a United States Major,
   who perhaps did not have to die.
The day after, Our Leader would properly mourn at the funeral of
   a woman of forty.
Within the following twenty-four hours, Lyndon Baines Johnson
   would show appropriate mortuary honor to a soldier of twenty
   years.
And so it would go on.
The idea of hell would be there, with its punishing recurrence, its
   reprimanding persistence.
Lyndon Baines Johnson has gone to the funeral of Francis Joseph
   Spellman, Cardinal Spellman.
The presence of Our Leader at this funeral should be only a
   beginning.

September Day

One could say Letty was tired,
As the city was dim,
And September mist was near at 6 o'clock.
Such hurrying on streets by her
That afternoon; such going up of steps.
Steps are present on week-days and a lot are gone up,
And Letty went up steps between 3 and 4.
Counters had her white hand
Resting on them in the afternoon,
Her hand later gloved.
By a ledger was the once skipping Letitia,
And the once sharply scolding Letitia,
Scolding a girl she knew.
So the tired Letitia is in the midst of a place growing darker,
Approaching a September night,
And in September darkening space;
Her eyes are now looking at windows,
Windows of a home,
Where on the range is burning
A plant; in a room's a fruit; on the range is burning
Flesh; and in a room is polished
Wood. The window's being seen
By fatigued, evening Letty.
Plate glass in daylight
And asphalt in afternoon city light.
And now, looking at the window
Of family-possessed apartment
By resting looker after dresses,
By Letitia Barnes at 6 o'clock,
Of a September day;
City September.

At Thermopylae, By Simonides of Ceos

O stranger, tell the Lacedaemonians
That we lie here, true to their laws.

38

Some Lines from Voltaire's Poem on the Disaster at Lisbon

1. Will You Say This?

Will you say, "It is the effect of everlasting laws
Which necessitates this choice by a free and good God"?
Will you say, seeing this heap of victims:
"God is avenged, their death is the payment of their crimes"?
What crimes, what bad things have been committed by these
    children,
Lying on the breasts of their mothers, flattened and bloody?
Lisbon, which is a city no longer, had it more vices
Than London, than Paris, given to doubtful delights?

2. We Are Not Oaks

If the eternal law which moves elemental things
Makes rocks fall, by the efforts of great winds,
If thickly growing oaks are burned by lightning—
They do not feel the blows which bring them down,
But I live; but I feel; but my heart, deeply hurt,
Asks for help from the God who made it exist.

3. God Is Asked About

What eye may see into his deep designs?
From a Being all perfect, evil cannot come to be.
It does not come from another, since God alone is master.
Yet, evil exists. O sad truths!
O astonishing mingling of contrarieties!
A God came to console our afflicted race;
He visited the earth, and has not changed it.

4. Why Cannot This Be?

Whatever opinion one has, one should shudder, no doubt.
There is nothing one knows, and nothing one does not question.
Nature is mute, she is questioned in vain.
There is need of a God who talks to humanity.
It is for him only to explain his work,
To console the weak, make the wise person clear.

5. *What Can Man Do?*

What can then do, the mind of largest range?
Nothing. The book of fate closes itself before our eyes.
Man, a stranger to himself, by man is not known.
What am I, where am I, where do I go, and from what do I come?
Atoms tormented on this mass of mud,
Whom death engulfs and with whom fate plays—
But thinking atoms, atoms whose eyes,
Guided by thought, have measured the skies.
From the very midst of the infinite, our lives go forth,
Without our being able, one moment, to see ourselves or know
    ourselves.

6. *Voltaire Tells of a Caliph*

A caliph once, at his last hour,
To the God whom he adored, said, for all prayer:
"I carry to you, O Only King, Only Unlimited Being,
All that which you don't have in your immensity—
Deficiencies, regrets, evils and ignorance."
But he might, also, have added: Hope.

7. *This Was Earlier in the Poem*

What is needed, O mortals? Mortals, it is needed that we suffer,
Submit ourselves silently, adore, and die.

8. *This Is in a Note*

O God, give us a Revelation that we should be humane and
    tolerant.

Stillness in the Field

In the stillness of the field
Lilies were growing;
In that stillness of the field
It was snowing
After days had gone.
The sun has come;
Clouds are with the sun;
And the hours go
One by one.

This Is Your Cup of Tea

The title has more than one meaning:
First, we're going to tell you about a cup of tea;
And then we're playing.

The cup of tea is from India, maybe,
And then it is right here.
This means it is foreign and domestic at once;
Away and immediate.

The tea flows
And there is the resisting and helping cup.
How firm the cup seems
Compared to the flexible, the liquid, the soft tea.
What could have more differing temperaments
Than a porcelain cup and flowing tea!

The cup, by itself, is down and up.
Good for the cup!

The cup, by itself, is severe,
What with its being hard.
However, it curves so gracefully.
The cup is severe and yielding.

The tea, the tea is there;
It remains;
It is still.
But we know the tea is in motion,
For it flows.
Stillness and motion,
In the same two seconds, Dwight!

The color of the tea is assertive
And also reclusive.
Boldness and modesty, Alice!

The cup has a center
On which a perpendicular line
Could rise.
Nevertheless, the cup is wide.
Verticality and horizontality and such, Euphemia!

Your cup of tea, then,
Is an arrangement
Of opposites, contraries, oppositions, polarities,
Contrasts, warrings, jars.
The cup is a series
Of reconciled jars.

This is your cup of tea:
A study in
The everlasting opposites.
Live with it, Horatio.
It is your cup of tea.

The Cydnus, By José Maria de Heredia

A wide, triumphant blue, a dazzling sun:
The silver trireme pales the river's flow:
And incense rises as the rowers row,
And flutes are heard as silken shivers run.

By pompous prow the fair and hawklike One
Leans out from royal place to see and know.
This Cleopatra proud, in evening show,
Seems like a mighty bird, with hunt begun.

In Tarsus waits a soldier's quiet face.
And ancient Egypt's queen, in eager space
Spreads out her amber arms—in purple, bright.
She has not seen, as sign of asking fate,
The godlike children whirl in subtle light:
Desire, Death. They play; they won't be late.

The Greatest Chinese
Name in the World

Me
Too.

Heaven for the Landlord; or,
Forthwith Understands

The landlord's Heaven is where
  There's a constant coming in of rent
  And nothing at all is spent
On any repair.

The landlord's Heaven is where
  As the Heavenly clouds roll—
  For him, rent increases roll
In, constantly; for there
Is no Heavenly rent control,
No Heavenly rent control—
Nothing to question the landlord's soul,
Nothing to question the landlord's soul.

What landlord ever to heaven went
Without a hope of collecting rent?—
Where the Heavenly clouds roll,
Where the rent increases roll
  Into the landlord's hands
  By the Great Landlord's clear commands—
Which every tenant understands:
Forthwith.

The Milkmaid and the Pot of Milk,
By Jean de La Fontaine

Perrette, having a pot of milk on her head,
Well-placed on a little cushion,
Thought how she would come without hindrance to the town.
In a light and short dress, she went with long strides,
Having put on that day, so that she would be more nimble,
A simple petticoat and flat shoes.
Our milkmaid so attired
Counted already in her thought
The price she got for her milk; used the money;
Bought a hundred eggs; had a triple brood of chickens.
Everything went well because of her constant care.

It is, she said, easy for me
To raise chickens about my house.
The fox will be very clever
If he doesn't leave me enough to have a pig.
The porker to become fat won't take much bran;
He was, when I got him, of reasonable weight:
I will have, when I sell him, fine and good money.
And who can stop me from putting in our stable,
Seeing how much money I will have, a cow and her calf,
Whom I will see leap about in the midst of a herd?
Perrette, as she thought this, leaps also, carried away:
The milk falls; goodbye calf, cow, pig, brood of chickens.
The lady-owner of all these good things, leaving with troubled eye
Her fortune so spread out,
Goes to excuse herself to her husband,
With a good chance of getting some blows.
The story was made into a little comedy:
It was called the Pot of Milk.
What mind doesn't wander over meadows?
Who does not build castles in Spain?
Picrochole, Pyrrhus, the milkmaid, everybody,
Wise men as well as fools.
Everybody dreams awake; there is nothing sweeter:
A soothing error carries away our minds,
All the riches of the world are ours,
All the honors, all the women.
When I am alone, I defy the most formidable person,
I travel, I put the Persian King off his throne,
I am elected King, my people love me;
Crowns are raining on my head.
Something happens, and I come back to myself:
I am John Smith as before.

They Look at Us

Martin Luther King
Is with John Brown.
Look up: you'll see them both
Looking down—
Deep and so wide
At us.

Happiness, By Arthur Rimbaud

O seasons, O castles,
What mind is without lack?

I have taken part in the magic study
Of happiness, a study no one can keep from.

Salute to it, each time
The French cock crows.

Ah, I want no more irritating againstness:
It has burdened my life.

That charm has taken self and body
And scatters energy.

O seasons, O castles.

The hour of flight, alas,
Will be the hour of surrender in death.

O seasons, O castles.

The Town Called Sleep

The dead approach a town called Sleep
Which is looking for them to be improved by.
For when the dead arrive, it takes on more—indeed, many—
    hilarious forms
And is a scene of immediate, wise revelry.
The wisdom that takes place when the dead arrive,
Is shockingly great, agreeably shocking.
There is no need to pity the dead.
They are very busy bringing out the possibility of the items of
    reality,
More—clearly—than in all reference books put together.
The patronizing of the dead must stop.
They aren't immortal—that's not the word: they are busy;
Cultivating wisdom, extending, increasing hilarity,
Nicely renovating the town called Sleep.

The Whale

Living through the ocean and in it, a big animal
Goes through days and hours and through time, until
Its shape of life changes altogether, and it dies.
It goes deep into green waters, and from their depths
Where is food for it, it takes for its living
Those things its needs make it to.

It goes through the minutes and hours all beings do and man;
And all things differently. It is a strange being, for nature
Has given the seas none like it so big and acting so.

There Is the Vivacious John Randle of Doylestown, Pennsylvania, 1817: A Found Poem

"Just as the twig is bent the TREE's inclined."

JOHN RANDLE
Informs his friends and the Public in general
That he has taken shelter under the
GREEN TREE,
Lately occupied by Daniel Woodruff,
Where he would be happy to accommodate all
Who may seek respite under its branches,
With the CHOICEST LIQUORS,
And best Provisions.

Desirous also, as well to CLOTHE
The naked as FEED
The hungry, he will likewise carry on the
TAILORING BUSINESS,
And trusts that by industry and attention
He will merit a share of public patronage.
April 8.

[*Doylestown Democrat*, April 29, 1817]

46

The Story of the French Revolution

For many years,
There was no French Revolution.
Then, look!
There was a French Revolution.

The Resolution of Conflict in Self Is Like the Making One of Opposites in Art. —Eli Siegel, 1941: Its First Form in a Chinese Manuscript, Circa, 250 B.C.

There is Reconciliation:
Which is the Way.
There is Self
Which is the Way.
There are Opposites
Which show the Way;
And are Art,
For they show the Way.
The true disciple
Makes one
Of the Way and what is not the Way:
This is the Way.
He who forgets Conflict
Forgets the Way.
What is the meaning of In?—
It is the Not-Absence of the Way.
The Reconciliation,
The Conflict,
These in self
Hint of the Flower
Which is the Way;
And of the not-flower
Which is the Not-Absence of the Way.
He who is in the Way
Thinks he is Everywhere Else.
And the Everywhere Else
Is the true Making One of the True Disciple.

47

This Seen Now

This seen now: a fly
Is all the world to a fly,
And a lady crossing a street
Is all there is, has been ever
To lady doing the crossing.
And the world has so many,
Many, many
Flies and ladies,
Crossing streets, ladies, flies.

These Are Five Haikus

1. Reality's Doing

We are then nearer
To what we were hoping for.
Reality's doing.

2. The Daisy Yesterday

The daisy is where it
Was, afternoon yesterday,
Shadows attending.

3. The Spoon

The spoon lying there
Has a ceiling over it
Spreading to window.

4. They Tell the Sky

The grass, the river
In unison tell the sky
It is high, rightly.

5. In Terror, Cockroach

The cockroach in terror
Crossed the rim of the whiteness
Maybe to safety.

48

To Dwight D. Eisenhower, with the Presence of Hart Crane and Antonin Artaud

You are the nave of a broken down church,
Whose architrave
Once giant rooks went off with
And gave it a false Our Lady of the Sorrows.
The wrinklings of the hour,
And the fraudulent corrugations of a cube
Are immersed in your ethos.
Mediaeval thus
Rises to the Romanesque
Of new evil by the Missouri.
You have spread desolation in Leuctra.
Epaminondas despises you,
And a small river near the Ilissus
Comprehends and corroborates.
Backs are turned on you
In unknown times.
The backs are charismatic.

While Two Shots in Spring

While two shots blazed nearly at once, killing one man, spring was
    coming along correctly in Wyoming.
The killed man, when the shot reached him, and went in him, lay
    down on the new, early spring grass, with a bullet near the
    fresh, green Wyoming grass.
The sun said not a word.
Not a coyote howled.
The killing man went off.
The killed man lay still.
Still with us, we have Wyoming, the sun, grass, coyotes, and ever
    so many springs.
The dead man lay still and the grass and sun went along quietly.
So did the bullets.
So did spring.
Let bullets follow their accustomed courses,
As they will, as they will.

Wove

This is what of
It was wove.

Rhymed Couplet

After having been among the trellis-work,
He found he had got dew on his shoes.

This The Egoist *Will Do: A Found Poem*

THE EGOIST.

This journal is NOT
A chatty literary review;
Its mission is NOT
To divert and amuse;
It is NOT
Written for tired and depressed people.
Its aim is rather
To secure a fit audience
And to render available
To that audience
Contemporary literary work
Bearing the stamp
Of originality and permanence;
To present *in its making*
Those contemporary literary efforts
Which ultimately will constitute
20th century literature.

The philosophical articles which THE EGOIST publishes,
By presenting the subject mater of metaphysics in a form
Which admits of logical treatment,
Are promising a new era for philosophy.
The power of its fictional work
Is investing that commonest but laxest form—

The novel as written in English,
With a new destiny and meaning.
In poetry, its pages
Are open to experiments
Which are transforming the whole conception of poetic form,
While among its writers appear
Leaders in pioneering methods
Radically affecting the allied arts.

Obviously a journal of interest to virile readers only.
Such should write, enclosing subscription, to:

THE EGOIST,
23 Adelphi Terrace House, Robert St., London, W.C. 2.

Published monthly.

Price, fifteen cents a number. Yearly subscriptions, one dollar sixty
  cents.

[*Poetry*, February, 1918]

This Is History

When rose petals, sometimes in night, go down through the air of
  night to grassed earth, green earth,
History is being made, history is not adequate without the doings
  of roses.
Roses have their ways, and rose petals have, and the fate of roses
  and rose petals, the leaving by rose petals of their roses, or
  their staying with their roses, the roses they, by nature's doing,
  belong to, is, truly, in history.
It may be that the same night, the same quiet, clean night, rose
  petals leave roses for earth, ships wash heavily, quietly against
  heavy, black waves, far out in large seas.
And waves, heavy, black and far, are, also, in history.
History takes in all the beautiful, all the exquisite, all the far; all
  great and sweet doings.
This is history.
This is history.

Helicopter Explains

I was a helicopter.
I was used in Vietnam.
They say I was shot down.
This is not so.
I didn't like what I was doing—
Stopping Vietnamese from having their land.
Not liking what I was doing,
I, a helicopter, fell.
So I was a helicopter.

The Expiation: I; By Victor Hugo

It snowed. Someone was defeated by his conquering.
For the first time, the eagle lowered its head.
Heavy days! The emperor came back slowly,
Letting Moscow in smoke burn behind him.
It snowed. The sharp winter came upon one, tumblingly.
After that white plain, another white plain.
Unrecognized now, chiefs and banners.
Yesterday *la grande armée* and now a flock of something.
Wings and centre were no longer told apart.
It snowed. The wounded hid themselves in the bellies
Of dead horses; at the edge of deserted encampments
You might see trumpeters frozen to their post,
Remaining upright, caparisoned and still, white in frost,
Sticking their stony mouths to trumpets of copper.
Bullets, grapeshot, shells, mixed with white flakes,
Fell down; grenadiers, surprised that they were trembling,
Marched in thought, ice at their grey moustaches.
It snowed. It snowed always! The cold wind
Whistled. A surface of frozen rain, in some dim place—
Men walked on this with bare feet and without food.
These were no longer living hearts, folk of war.
It was a dream wandering in cold haze, a mystery,
A procession of shades under a black sky.
The vast loneliness, fearful to look at,
Everywhere appeared: a mute avenger.
The sky made noiselessly of the thick snow

An immense shroud for this army;
And everyone, feeling death was present, was alone.
—Will one ever get from out this deadly empire?
Two enemies! The czar, the north. The north is worse.
Men discarded cannon to burn the gun-carriages.
Who lay down, died. A group sad and confused:
They fled: the desert devoured the line.
You were able through folds which the snow raised
To see that regiments had gone to sleep there.
O defeats of Hannibal! tomorrows of Attila!
Runaways, wounded, dying, caissons, handcarts, litters,
These crowded at bridges in order to cross rivers.
Ten thousand went to sleep, a hundred waked.
Ney, whom an army followed a while ago, now
Got away, fighting for his watch with three Cossacks.
Every night: Qui-vive! Watch! Assaults! Attacks!
—These phantoms take their guns, and on them
They see rush, frightening, darksome—
With cries like the voices of bald vultures—
Horrible squadrons, whirls of fierce men.
A whole army in this way lost itself in the night.
The emperor was there, upright, looking.
He was like a tree given over to the ax.
On this giant, grandeur spared until then,
Unhappiness, sinister woodman, had mounted;
And he, living oak, insulted by the hatchet,
Trembling under a spectre of dreary retaliations,
Watched his branches fall about him.
Leaders, soldiers, all died. Each had his turn.
While surrounding his tent lovingly,
Some saw his shadow go and come on the cloth surface:
(These were they who remained, and, believing always in his star,
Accused destiny of a deep insult to greatness).
He felt suddenly his very being frightened.
Stupefied by disaster, and not knowing what to believe,
The emperor looked towards God; the man of glory
Trembled; Napoleon saw that he was expiating
Something, perhaps; and, leaden-colored, disquieted,
Before his legions strewn on the snow:
Is it my punishment, he says, God of armies?
Then he hears himself called by name
And someone speaking to him in the shadows, says: No.

The Stars That Summer

The stars
Told their meaning steadily
All that summer.

We Have Had with Us This Sun

This day, this,
Drearily came the sun to the world,
With beds everywhere in the world.
Such beds, such uses of beds, at 7:10 A.M., November.
The big sun, in its well-known way, came, let happen what may to
anyone, in this world spoken of.
The sun makes beds alight: before they were in dark, and everywhere
from beds come persons who through hours of night, with the
sun otherwise, had to do with sleep in many ways, each for
himself and herself.
Sleep never comes the same way to anyone.
As mists were leaving earth, and this November day was growing
more light, plainly, and beds no longer had so many people
with them, the sun was growing older, hours older; we have
with us a changing, more mature sun all the while.
Jennie, Agnes, John, Ethel, Mr. Swithens, April Entwhistle, June
Dedham, Molly Graves all saw the sun this November morning,
and all had something or other done to them by the busy,
important, effective sun.
Agnes was dealt with so by the sun; Mr. Swithens (Edgar Swithens)
so; Miss April Entwhistle seeing the sun had something done to
her; and so did many, many Miss Aprils; same with many, many
Miss Junes, and surely with Miss Marys, Helens, Doras and
Ediths, and, well, Eleanors, too.
Constantly, the sun is doing things to humans; constantly, the sun
is doing things to mists and various ladies, girls, men, boys,
women and the like in this earth somewhere in things.
And so did this sun, coming in the sun's way, this 7:10 A.M., this
November morning.
We have with us this sun.
We have had with us this sun.
We have had with us this sun.

54

To a Slushy Pear

I address you, O slushy pear.
I say, even, Hail, O slushy pear,
And think it is correct—
As once in the 17th century and in the 18th century the sunrise
    was hailed; morn, light, deity.
For one thing, the sun was present in your coming to be, O slushy
    pear.
And light is with your brown covering, now protecting unhandsome
    softness like the softness of some flesh giving sorrow to those
    who have it.
Even as you are slushy, there is the eminent pear contour, with
    narrowness and wideness so unerringly and gently going on;
    and boldly too.
There is all that was needed for you to exist, O slushy pear.
First, there was a tree: definitely a pear tree.
Second, there was land.
Third, there was warmth—with the sun there, O slushy pear.
Gad, what chemistry is fourth: chemistry blatantly and hiddenly
    proceeding.
For you to be slushy, much had to be likewise.
And you are slushy.
I can think of some pears, green and hard, and you withdraw
    viscidly; you take on softness, crushability, wetness and such.
Slush is a composite of non-dry manifestations.
Behold, now, there is your core.
Your core, though wet, is an arrangement.
The arrangement hasn't been wholly explained yet.

II

Ethics can be found in you, O slushy pear.
Forlornness and sadness are yours.
But you don't seem to have any plan.
The evil is on the side of sorrow.
And you are sweet.
This can be ascertained.

III

Slushy pear, you are a thing,
And I give you the homage a thing deserves.
It must be so.

A Lady, Sun and Rain

In the world, of that year,
A lady living in a quiet street of a city rather large,
Looked at the sun after rain,
And then thought of conditions in her home.
She was pretty,
And she hadn't liked the rain.
And now a wind came,
And blew wet green leaves, and twigs, and other things along the wet
    street.
O lady, thinking of conditions in the home,
Who didn't like the rain,
Though you are pretty,
O lady, O lady,
Rain is in the world,
And the sun is in the world,
Along with conditions in the home;
And rain is beautiful, and the sun is beautiful,
And more.

L. B. Johnson Should Be Given All Time to Understand the Pain He Has Caused

We hope that L. B. Johnson is immortal.
It is only by being immortal that he can find out how much pain he
    has caused.
With an endless number of days, he can understand how unjust he
    has been.
With an immeasurable life, Johnson can find all the wrong he has
    permitted, the injury he has encouraged.
God asks us that we understand where we have done wrong.
God wishes that we understand, see all that we have done which is
    not good.
Immortality is for the understanding of the unjust.
Why should not L. B. Johnson, who became President of the United
    States some years ago, be immortal?
It does seem to us divine propriety.

Address to Death Acknowledging Its Full Presence

Death is something that can come to Kentucky,
And lay low girl in orange dress, busied a little with chemistry of a
  hundred and more years ago.
It comes where glass is, tubes are; is present between walls, and
  above the last branches of trees.
Kentucky has had it often; bodies are there visited by the visiting,
  meetable, wishable death.
Death, you are as good as white, fast waves and confusion at two.
You have it over misery and dust coming from shelves to outside
  cars.
This is a hymn to you and it is expected you will acknowledge it
  some crowded summer.
Furnished you are with the means of terrifying, freezing, dividing,
  mouldering.
This shows that you are rich in action, diverse in manner of coming.
Say that Kentucky scorns—say that it does; it is well for you.
Come suddenly high in air and make topple the stammerer, crumple
  the halter, crash against the hesitating.
It is well, bright and gray.
And Kentucky is gray and many.
This having been seen, go to some other town.
Desired and invisible,
Solid and desired,
Talked of death.
And later, more of death, more of it, and gray and brightness and
  crashing of hammers, their falling, and the persistence of gray
  to the east.

Anonymous Anthropology

Anthropology deals with people anonymously,
None of whom we know individually.
We don't know a specific person as to pottery, textiles, utensils,
  bronze or stone.
Anthropology, which is in league with prehistory,
Is so anonymous, we don't know how sad we feel about it,
Until we think about it.

Frankie and Johnny, Changed by a Malign Spirit into Dorry and Johnnie, with Words on Aesthetic Realism, the Opposites, the Terrain Gallery, Purpose B and the Hope of Man

Dorry and Johnnie were nudniks,
  Oh, but they could hide.
They swore to be true to each other,
  And put everything else aside.

> *Chorus.*   They were mighty clever,
>   But they weren't that good.

Dorry went out with her scissors,
  Johnnie went out with his glue,
All for to be cuttin' and smotherin'
  Something not theirs and new.

> *Chorus.*   They were mighty clever,
>   But they weren't that good.

No matter how big your position,
  No matter how high you're up there,
If there's something around worth studyin'
  You have to be modest and fair.

> *Chorus.*   You're mighty clever,
>   But you're not that good.

Bring out your rubber-tired carriages,
  Bring out your critical hacks,
'Cause you can't be hurtin' the opposites,
  And you can't be changin' the facts.

> *Chorus.*   They were mighty clever,
>   But they weren't that good.

Through Winds

Oh, you would cry, tree in autumn,
As the wind went through you that October,
With green under you and the wind.
You would cry, tree in autumn,
Where once, led by her father, going west,
A child moaned a little, fidgeting.
O, tree of Missouri,
O, tree of autumn in Missouri,
Some years ago,
With every autumn you cry, with every autumn winds go through
    you.
You would cry, for so are things, so is existence, so are you, so
    am I.
And the little child came to Oregon, from Kentucky, through
    Missouri, through autumn, through winds.

Mourn This Sparrow, By Gaius Valerius Catullus

Mourn, O Graces and Loves,
And those men who are of the Graces:
The sparrow is dead, of my girl,
The sparrow, delight of my girl,
Whom she loved more than her eyes.
For sweet was his way with her,
And he knew her as well as a girl her mother.
Nor would he move from her lap—
But, hopping this way and that way,
Would sing for his lady alone.
Now he goes on the dark path,
The one, it is said, no one comes back from.
Evil be with you, evil darknesses
Of Orcus, who swallow all beautiful!
For you have taken from me my lovely sparrow.
Ah, unkind doing! Ah, poor sparrow!
It is your work, that, of my girl,
The eyes are red and heavy with weeping.

My Ranch: A Composition by Our Leader, Lyndon Baines Johnson

I have a ranch.
Most people know this, but what they may not know is how my
  ranch agrees with me.
There are many acres in this ranch—
And every one of them sees the foreign situation my way.
How fine it is,
While riding or walking
On the acres of my ranch,
To see the grass looking up at me,
And contented.

I get inspiration from the grass on the acres of my ranch.
I hear no harsh word from a single blade.
If I walk on the grass, the grass seems to understand.
If I ride on the grass, I do not hear the jarring sound of ill-advised
  criticism.

That is why I love my ranch in all its acres.
I'm sure you would, too, if you found the deep satisfaction in your
  ranch that I do in mine.
Only from the grass
On the acres of a ranch
Do you get true understanding,
True cooperation.

And so, after having been a while on the acres of my ranch,
I come back to Washington or elsewhere—
And am able to make the criticism of me meaningless:
With my poise and my unperturbed sense of value.
I am quite sure
That were it not for my ranch,
People would notice a faltering
In my insight and determination.

Summing up, then,
I bring this composition
To a close
By saying:

If you have a ranch,
And you know how to benefit
From the cooperation
Of the acres and the grass,
Ill-advised, uninformed criticism
Will not disturb you
A whit,
A jot,
A quaver.

End of composition
By Our Leader.

Cue from Cuba

Take a cue from Cuba,
It won't Costa Rica.
Why be Chile
When you got new Colombia?
You Guatemala
Where you want them; and you can Panama.
There will be nothing to Peru.
There is no need to Venezuela.
There is a better way to Bolivia.
There is something to El Salvador
And to Ecuador.
The new way will Honduras long as its rightness;
Living doesn't have to be with such slim Argentina.
So don't Brazil.
Fidel is a good Paraguay,
And a good Uruguay.
He is showing us where to Mexico,
What we Dominican Republic.
We should be most Puerto Rico for the different.
There is no reason we should Haiti ourselves.
Time and justice have their Nicaragua.

Take a cue from Cuba,
It won't Costa Rica.

Earth, 1920

Earth, after many years,
Through her tears,
Looks in her glass.
And she thus appears:
Most of her dark, alas;
But here and there, a mass
Of light, which this dark fears.

Hymn to Jazz and the Like

What is sound, as standing for the world and the mind of man at
any time, and in any situation?
Sound is an unknown, immeasurable reservoir which has been
gone into and used to have chants, rituals, jigs, bourrées,
sonatas, symphonies, songs, concertos: all of these show
themselves, proudly saying, I am sound, I am music.
Sound took a new form in America or somewhere, Oh, say, around
1900.
There had been Go Down, Moses, which did new, clattering,
ominous, delightful, religious, thundering, kind things with
sound.
There had been Never Said a Mumblin' Word, which did things
with sound different from what occurred in Don Giovanni,
Xerxes, or The Bohemian Girl—you know, The Bohemian
Girl of Balfe.
Sound is looking for new illustrations showing the might, glory,
findingness, and abandon of man.
Yah, and Oh, Lord, there was the St. Louis Blues.
Sounds were made to fall into different places in this.
Notes behaved otherwise.
Something in you expected a note here, and it was there.
Something in you expected a note to be this way and it was that.
Ha, what Jazz does to the this and that of notes, the isness and
wasness and might-be-ness of chords.
Frankie and Johnnie was notes doing different things in America,
being in front of each other and in back of each other
differently,
Being large and small differently.
Ah, what a blessing in rowdy divinity Casey Jones is!

She'll Be Coming Round the Mountain helped to have notes show
more of what they could do.
And there was Alexander's Ragtime Band.
(Berlin, Irving first name, was proximate to the right wildness then.)
And, Venus Anadyomene, the Beale Street Blues, with its going
down and up and around,
And its sassy tragedy.
And let's mention Memphis Blues.
East St. Louis Toodle-O, go into dark, make advanced noise there,
moan with grandeur, and come out right.
The Mooche, you come like a procession of right people at twilight
saying, This is right, not that; and you walk against walls and
the walls run.
In the Mood, Glenn Miller or no, you show what repetition can
do and surprise like the surprise in Beethoven's Emperor
Concerto as it changes from a hush and faintness to crash.
In the Mood, you are acclaimed.
Fletcher Henderson, when you brought scholarship to the new
joyous earth-turning in America, you did something for Jazz
and destiny's certificate.
The Music Goes Round and Round—whatever you come from, you
do something for reality as center and circumstance, sober
whirling, valve majesty, surprise and the heaven of brashness.
Jazz, you have faltered, but it was you who faltered, and there was
you.
Jazz, you show that symmetry and unsymmetry, order and casualness
are alike.
The Beatles have used you somewhat to show that the whisper of
one person can shout across land and water.
Rock and Roll, you say something of geology and man's
uncertainty.
Jazz, you are amiable about Chopin's Revolutionary Etude.
Jazz, when Mozart was most vocally bold in the Don Giovanni, you
were looking on years ago, ready to be encouraged honorably.
Jazz, you were around when the Gregorian Chant was doing things
to man somewhat after Charlemagne and after the changing of
France to a kingdom.
Jazz, you have in you Homer, Marlowe, Coleridge, Kipling,
Swinburne, Hopkins, Rimbaud, also the person who wrote Sir
Patrick Spens.
(I am not being careless.)
Jazz, you deserve another hymn.

Death's Intention and Opposition Thereto, 1861

Two young men rode and rode
As part of a Civil War episode.

Green leaves rustle, as green leaves do—
Now when the Civil War is new.

Death is ready, as usual, to go forth
And visit, indiscriminately, south and north.

Death has grieved, but never grieves
That wise leaf among the rustling leaves.

Death will shock, but will not shock
That wise leaf by the Rappahannock.

Fare Thee Well

Oh, mighty America, hast thou come to this?
Has all thy grandeur, all thy hopes, all thy wonder,
Thy Bradford and thy Franklin,
Thy Whitman and thy Boone,
Thy Cooper and thy Norris,
Thy London and thy Debs,
Thy Jane Addams and thy sunrise—
Come to this?
That thou shouldst be looked on with terror
By an unknown child in Asia?—
Fare thee well, O land, fare thee other.

I Am So Glad I Am Not Fulton Lewis Jr.'s Niece

I am so glad I am not Fulton Lewis Jr.'s niece.
Much has happened to me I can scream about.
I have been piggish too, and barrenly uncooperative with my
    friends.
I have failed to call up people whom I promised I would call up.
I have made scenes at parties, in which I threw ashtrays out of
    windows, at mirrors, and when I was subsiding, at couches.

My grandfather was accused of manipulating stocks improperly.
My great-aunt used to read horrible, vacuous fiction hour after
  hour on Southern piazzas.
So I am glad I am not Fulton Lewis Jr.'s niece.
Once a friend saw me punching myself in the belly just over the
  navel,
Because I suddenly remembered my Presbyterian days and thought
  punching my navel was a good way of acknowledging the
  divine displeasure with me, my thoughts, my activities, and my
  outlook.
I once took a jar of strawberry jelly and, because I didn't like the
  way the grocery clerk talked to me, emptied it on the counter
  slowly but thoroughly, and walked out with a look at the
  counter clerk who just before had been adjusting a shelf.
The way I impressed him can surely not be measured.
It is one of my victories I remember as if it were an ethical etching
  or a color print, clear as anything.
Lord, those strawberries oozing uncertainly and slowly on the
  counter!
So you see I am glad I am not Fulton Lewis Jr.'s niece.
If you are not Fulton Lewis Jr.'s niece, you have something to
  begin with, a little sliver of light in the otherwise dim, murky,
  thick surroundings for self.
Perhaps I am the only girl in America who fully appreciates not
  being Fulton Lewis Jr.'s niece.
This is because of my past and my fits.
When Fulton Lewis Jr. has a fit, it comes out soft, the way my
  strawberries did.
My fits are real and sharp.
Fulton Lewis Jr. is against things, but he oozes, is viscous, is heavy
  with personal moist superfluity.
I have had my fits straight.
Perhaps, even, I won't have any, one of these years.
With all this, I have to say again:
I am so glad I am not Fulton Lewis Jr.'s niece.

In a Painting

In a painting you can twist
Toast.

Carry Me Away, By Henri Michaux

Carry me away into a Portuguese boat of once,
Into an old and gentle Portuguese boat of once,
Into the stem of the boat, or if you wish, into the foam,
And lose me, in the distance, in the distance.

Into the yoking of another time.
Into the deceiving velvet of snow.
Into the breath of some dogs brought together again.
Into the weary gathering of dead leaves.

Carry me, without breaking me, into kisses,
Into breasts that raise themselves and breathe,
On palms covering them and their smile,
Into the corridors of long bones, and of articulations.

Carry me away, or rather dig me deep.

Come, Spring Flowers

Though the whole world will work to make you to,
I say, Come, spring flowers.

Gluck Found Unidentified Flying Objects and You Can Hear Them in His Orfeo

I am more interested in Gluck's *Orfeo* than in Unidentified Flying
Objects.
The Musical Composer looks for unidentified flying objects in space,
and, finding them, he has them become notes which others can
play.
Once Gluck's *Orfeo* consisted of unidentified flying objects no one
had found yet, knew about, got together.
Gluck found these, and some of them are in his *Orfeo.*
We can hear them now.
They are Identified Flying Objects: notes, chords, bars, phrases,
cadences.
Unidentified Flying Objects which land on earth and are not the
instances music needs, may as well be unidentified, say I in a
motion of indifference.

Humanity

Arthur looks to the next day with some foreboding,
As Barbara is pleased to give up a dear friend.
Cornelia is forgotten, for she lived long ago.
Dave is after money, but he wants children, too, and an obedient
   wife.
Edward is afraid of so many things, it is hard to say what he wants
   strongly.
Frank takes things as they come, except when he can't.
A thing can frighten Gertrude, which she hardly sees.
When you say things to Hulbert, you can be hardly sure he's
   listening.
If you hear a mean thing from Ingrid, do not be surprised.
Jacqueline gets confused, but she manages to hide it pretty well.
Kenneth is ambitious, but he has fits of awful laziness.
Louis does pretty well, but he is not too clear about what is
   important.
Manny's fondness for money is excessive.
Nona is in delicate health, and doesn't like people.
Ottfried lived long ago, and so he should not get into this at all.
Paul can change his mind without knowing it.
Quincy is given to intellectual things in order to live up to his
   name; but he has an interesting, in fact inordinate, fondness for
   sweets.
Rachel has a tendency to be sad in a manner which is discomforting
   to those close to her.
Sidney wishes to go into politics, and his desire for political success
   is so great, other things some people are fond of are not to be
   looked for in him, or shall we say, from him.
Thomas is dull as a means of protecting himself.
Ursula is a nun at heart, without being too religious; she is a
   paradox persons haven't found it zestful enough to understand.
Viola in a dim way is given to everything musical, but eating is
   attractive, too, to her.
Winnie is frivolous as a means of conquering life.
Ximena is a nice name, but there is no girl to go with it.
Yolanda coughs a great deal to hide her continuing uncertainty
   about life.
Zoë is passionate, but it is not for life.
These are people picked purposefully but representative all.
Watch out, watch out, and see into what category you may fall.
And you will, you will, unless you are critical.

Decision: A Wildflower

Decision is a wildflower
In the field of habit.

July Room

Ah, the moon is present in the room
Amid the chandeliers and watched by old men.
The old men are not tired of watching the moon,
Though wars have palled on them.
Some of them have seen 2,000 daffodils,
Eight hundred or so in America.
And their minds have gone from daffodils to moons,
Blithely. For they are old men and the world
Comes to them with sweet fragmentariness,
As it has come. They are not tired of kissing the hands
Of titled blondes, though some have never kissed
Such hands; at least they do not remember to have done just such
    kissing.
It has been a fight with the old men of daffodils being seen and
    skins being kissed,
And I believe the daffodils won. But right now the old men are
    not tired of seeing the frequent and unfragmentary moon
Merging with the chandeliers of a July room.

A Need by Philosophy, A Passage of Kant, In Lines: A Found Poem

There is a need
By philosophy
Of a science
Which shall determine
The possibility, principles, extent
Of human knowledge
À priori.

Of far more importance
Than all that has been said above

68

Is the consideration
That certain of our cognitions
Rise completely above
The sphere
Of all possible experience,
And by means of conceptions,
To which there exists
In the whole extent of experience
No corresponding object,
Seem to extend
The range of our judgments
Beyond its bounds.

[Kant: *Critique of Pure Reason*. Introduction, Section III.]

She Is Waiting, Dear Hippolita

She was the dreariest girl in the world, and her name was Hippolita.
She was so dreary in her own company, she had to be a gadabout.
The things she said to herself were of such a kind, no one would
     talk to her, if she said them to other people.
Any day, you may meet Hippolita.
She is waiting.

II

If you just talk to her, she thinks you are making fun of her.
If you are silent, she thinks you are ridiculing her.
If, however, you praise her, she thinks more than ever you are
     making fun of her.

III

Even so, she is waiting.
She wants to meet you.
No matter who you are, she likes your company more than her own.

IV

She is dear, dreary, waiting Hippolita.

69

Logic, Roses and Red

Roses in the world,
World's things,
Red, say, like sunsets,
Say, like Indians are said to be in some books.
Roses, how often it has been said, are red.
Red is the world then, for roses which are the world's, are red.
Logic has to do with roses, and doesn't it, though.
Logic is a mighty thing, mighty in beauty, and logic is in roses,
and logic and beauty go together.
Logic is in roses, logic is in red; roses are in the world, and it's true.
Red roses are in the world; logic, roses and red.

Payment for Honesty;
or, A Family How Impelled?

"There's a whole bunch of them—Aesthetic Realist painters I mean
—a bunch of kooks, I've met them all. There's this couple called
Dorothy and Chaim Koppelman, who are the spokesmen for the
painting gang."
—*New York, Sunday Herald Tribune,* July 26, 1964

There have been all kinds of injustice in this world, for man, his
self not big enough, or entire, is given to injustice.
We can hurt at night with our hands and weapons, and we can be
unwilling to see causes.
In that territory which is injustice, mental enclosedness and the
horrible are not so far away.
Here, in New York, we have the question: Why are Dorothy,
Chaim, and Ann Koppelman so busy in behalf of a way of
looking at the world,
Which, O City Editors, is called Aesthetic Realism, and is seen as
of Eli Siegel?
Not to want to know why, fairly, is that mental indolence, that
harsh enclosedness of self which, in the territory of the
visible, makes for horrible little pieces in the columns of our
papers.
Dishonoring the feelings of others, not wanting to know what is
cause in them, what is in their minds saliently and deeply

Is with attacking the bodies of others, we being enraged at a
    depriving world.
Is it possible that the Koppelmans care for what they do care for
    because they saw, and the largeness in their minds made them
    unable to do otherwise?
Are they arduous for the opposites in all the arts and in every man,
    because they saw the emergent truth of this for themselves?
Is it possible they were unwilling as anyone else to give themselves
    to a way of seeing presented by another?—
This, O gabblers at parties and functionaries amid the mass media,
    is to be considered.

II

Ann Koppelman, youthfully eminent at Brooklyn College, has
    been talked to greasily by professors.
Chaim Koppelman has been looked at doubtfully by fellow teachers
    of art.
Dorothy Koppelman has been gossiped about by art people for
    her fervency:
—Ludovico, wherefore this fervency?

III

It is time to see the impulsion of the Koppelmans truly.
It is an impulsion we want to have, with all our labyrinthine
    groovedness and slick temporizing.
Unwillingness, insincerity have been the Koppelmans', too.
Snobbishness has not exactly passed them by.
But now they are able to represent what is longed for by man—
    even on campuses, even in officies where copy is read.
There is a family of three which can be praised in America—
With the uncertain being what it is, and good and evil taking each
    other's places like thousands of bits of paper whirling for a
    long time in winds that do not stop.

The Waving of the Grain

In summer, the waving of the grain
In the western United States,
Is a sight, tinged with economics,
And prevailing for acres, miles.

Impassioned Lines Comprising a Tribute to the Historic Meaning of Bernard Goldfine

If others had not been foolish, we should be so.
—BLAKE, *Marriage of Heaven and Hell*

Anyone who can show
That behind the appearance
Of dour White Mountainness,
And behind the impressive, secret exercise of power, central power—
Lies the wrongly beating heart of acquisitiveness;
And the faint humanity of evasion—
This servant of truth,
This fighter in shadowy lists for the true relation of good and evil,
This fated warrior for the junction of surface and interiority—
Should be HONORED.
And this servant of Things and Their Truth
Is Bernard Goldfine of Boston.
He is of that people from which, it seems,
Spinoza arose;
Who with *more intent*
Worked for *that*
Which Bernard Goldfine, largely unknowingly,
Dazzlingly, recently worked for.

II

History, coyly perhaps,
(But it does)
Honors Mr. Goldfine of Boston.

Lovely Little Fisher Lad

I love a little fisher lad
  Living by the sea.
I love this little fisher lad,
  And I think he loves me.

Lovely little fisher lad,
  Living by the sea—
Tho' now I know you love me,
  Will you always love me?

72

Intactus; or, Nothing Doing

Out of the words they say of me,
Mean as a truth for one and all,
I thank whatever guile may be
For my unconquerable gall.

In the fell grip of all the facts,
I haven't seen or granted aught.
Amid my conscience and my acts,
My head is whirling, but untaught.

Beyond this place of just what's so,
Looms defeat for me and mine.
The fear of what I do not know
Dissolves in my eternal whine.

It matters not how great the truth,
How rich with newness all out there;
I'm in my own majestic booth,
I am the Colonel of my care.

Disclaimer of Prejudice

It's no use having good taste in Chicago.
You've got to change your city before it means anything.
This is not racial prejudice.
It's not your skin or your religion.
It's the city.

II

I've never been on State Street, Chicago,
And I've never dreamed of being on it.
All I've done is to read about people who have been on it and
    near it.
And I pitied them, always, a little.

III

So it's not your race,
Or your skin or your religion.
It's the city.

A Woeful Ballad on Faking Away

Drifting down the sea of Ego,
　　Faking away, faking away;
Postponing honesty interminably,
　　Faking away, faking away.

Being two people cleverly,
Maintaining narrative duality,
A thought for you, and one for me—
　　Faking away.

Changing story with geography,
Telling things dilutedly,
Showing no temerity,
Rather large timidity;
　　Faking away.

Telling of the story some,
Strategically acting dumb,
Half alive, half voluntarily numb:
　　Faking away, faking away.

General Westmoreland Wants Glory and Isn't Getting It: A Military Soliloquy

Here I am in Saigon and am about the most important person in
　　the place.
How I got here I don't know entirely; I'm not supposed to; I'm a
　　general; generals take orders, too.
Sometimes, I don't think I'm so bright the way some West Pointers
　　would see bright—let alone some Harvard fellows or Princeton.
If I think too much, I don't feel good; and besides it doesn't help
　　my military effectiveness.
(My military effectiveness; there's something—I love it, it explains
　　everything and makes me look good whatever I may be doing.
I wish everything was military; I'd feel surer.)
Well, I'm here in Saigon and though I don't know much about
　　these parts, as I say, I'm the most important person in it.

74

Even when somebody comes visiting—a senator friend or an
administration pal—I'm the most important person here; it's
my military look, you see: effectiveness.
—Those two guys, Thieu and Ky—some shady types; but we
need them.
You don't know what kind of guy you have to be nice to, as a part
of military effectiveness.
Strictly, those two—Ky and Thieu—are on the creepy side, like
some people's relatives.
I could go on thinking like this for days.
—But there's one thing—I don't have enough glory.
I mean glory—the kind you have parades for and people making
noise about.
Here I am in Saigon, the most important person in it, but I'm
almost a shut-in.
Where do I go in real style, with people excited, their hearts going
up and down?
I envy that northern Sherman: he went through South Carolina
after going through Georgia.
What in the name of anything do I go through?
My people don't like Sherman, but he was on the move.
When he burned Columbia, S.C., he was on the move.
Am I on the move?
What a situation for me—to be jealous of that Yankee Sherman.
—I have to be more important than ever looking at a map or getting
some detail.
—I'm tired a little and I find it hard to figure out why those dark
guys Thieu and Ky are on the creepy side.
And I was so clear only a short while ago.
—Damn it all: I want glory not just a build up and pictures—
though I must say I look handsome enough to make anyone
feel bad, and that's *something.*

Matter Moves on the Avenue

Matter moves on the avenue;
Gowns stir;
Dresses advance.

Sunlight in Slush, in Puddles, and in Wet Municipal Surfaces; or, Miracle on Eighth Avenue below Fourteenth Street

I

It was a dying sun, too.
The sun did not have the energy it had two hours ago, nor in some
days last June,
But it was the same sun, with the same distances.
—Was it the sun in black water
On an Eighth Avenue pavement?
What else could it be?
The sun was allotting itself to ever so many dark, watery surfaces;
I guess, being the sun, it could do nothing else.
But it was a miracle, a miracle being that you can look at, with
amazement inhabiting what you look with.
Certainly, it was before, but there was something like amazement
when the sun (they say it is millions of miles away) was,
through its light, in the consequences of a February rainfall
and snowfall at once, with warmth present.
The sun was in February slush.
If this is not something to be amazed at,
Let us consult the most incredible lives of saints,
Written carelessly,
And call ourselves not careful.

II

The sunlight was like a true saint, a factual saint,
As it took up residence in slush.
The sunlight was like a beneficent mediaeval visitation
As it took up discernible residence in a puddle.
One puddle, along with the sun, had clouds in it
As plain as anything:
Grey, rotund, white vagueness within a puddle of water.

III

It is necessary to say what sunlight in slush bodes.
Offhand, it seems hard to think it bodes anything but well.
Slush (undesirable) is visited with power by February sunlight
(desirable)
And the slush has it that way, by the nature of slushness.

IV

Slush is of various kinds,
Puddles are of various kinds.

Black wet areas on pavements
Are of various kinds:
But the February sunlight was present in all the kinds that came
   to be on Eighth Avenue below Fourteenth Street the day I'm
   speaking of.
The sunlight was present, even, in a furrow a car had made.
Sunlight gets into vehicular furrows and can be recorded as being
   in furrows.

V

The hardware store looked on.
Pizza selling went on near the visitation of slush by sunlight, and
   dwelling therein.
Sanctity can come to pizzas
As you think of sunlight—fading but there—in slush, some of it
   with long oblong furrows.

VI

While sunlight—dying sunlight—
Can come to slush,
We can't be sure
What can visit us,
What can occur to us;
What we are in a world of light without end
And possible slush ready to show itself, too—
In a world where both light and slush are indefatigable, and, are
   often friendly in February.

Spark

I am a spark,
Which always goes out,
For it needs another spark.
What is your name, bystander?
What is your name, wayfarer?

Putting on a Glove Did Something for You, Anyway

Not one glove
Protected a woman really
In the 1850's.
Gloves were put on,
And from Paris, too—
Some from London—
But the heart was as unknowing,
The blood was as uncertain,
The vistas of self as unclear.
Yet the putting on of a glove
Sustained a smile of victory,
Or amiable disdain,
Or just the smile for which it seemed
The moment had come.
You seemed to answer a question as you put on a glove.
It had to do.

The Albatross, By Charles Baudelaire

Often, to amuse themselves the men of the crew
Lay hold of the albatross, vast birds of the seas—
Who follow, sluggish companions of the voyage,
The ship gliding on the bitter gulfs.

Hardly have they placed them on the planks,
Than these kings of the azure, clumsy and shameful,
Let, piteously, their great wings in white,
Like oars, drag at their sides.

This winged traveler, how he is awkward and weak!
He, lately so handsome, how comic he is and uncomely!
Someone bothers his beak with a short pipe,
Another imitates, limping, the ill thing that flew!

The poet resembles the prince of the clouds
Who is friendly to the tempest and laughs at the bowman;
Banished to ground in the midst of hootings,
His wings, those of a giant, hinder him from walking.

The Reason for Sweetie, A Cat's, Leaving Us in May 1959

Last May—May 1959, Sweetie or Buzz, the cat long in our home,
Became free, and went elsewhere to do good deeds.
Her first great deed, at least the first we who are around have been
    able to notice,
Was the falling of a plane near Sverdlovsk, Russia, on May 1, 1960.
This happening put ethics in a true light in this United States,
    and showed people, having power, as having been bad with
    ethics for a long time.
These people whom Sweetie helped so much to discomfit and have
    recognized, can now do less harm.
They have been made less powerful as they have been made more
    ridiculous.
The world rejoices.
Sweetie has enabled the world honestly to rejoice.
All praise, then, to this cat, Sweetie or Buzz.

We now can take better her leaving; her leaving us.
We can see why.
The cause is so great and so fine, so effective, it successfully opposes
    our grief.
And Sweetie, we know, will do more.
The cat close to us will do much more that is good for everything.

Prayer of a Secretary of Defense in Pain

Lord, Thou hast twisted my ankle.
I suffer from the ankle which is twisted.
Suffering is pain, and man dislikes pain as he dislikes nothing else.
I have pain, and I do not like it.
It has been told me that I have helped cause pain to people I did
    not know,
In Asia; people who do not see the world as I do.
If their pain is like my pain, they do not like it either.
I have thought that they deserved their pain, these people who see
    the world in a way not like that, seemingly, of many Americans.
And the question comes—I do not want it to, but it comes: do I
    deserve my pain?

79

It is hard for anyone to think he deserves the pain he has.
I do not see myself as deserving the pain I have.
And I think of Asian people who apparently do not like me, and
    their pain.
I do not want to, but I do.
Lord, I even hear, see some Asians say that Thou hast given me
    this twisted ankle and its pain because of how I have dealt
    with them and talked of them.
When you have a twisted ankle, O Lord, you can think anything.
I do not want to, but I hear them.
They say: Thou, or a God who is like Thee, hast given me this
    twisted ankle to have me forbear from giving Asian people I
    do not know pain like mine.
I am compelled to say this, Lord.
Pain is so powerful.
Sometimes I think it is powerful the way Thou art.
Bitterly, O Lord, I ask Thee that something cease.

I Should Love to Be Loved, By Endre Ady

From a French translation of Endre Ady's Hungarian lyric in *Les Cinq Continents*, ed. Goll. Translators: Sandor Eckhardt and Zoltan Baranyi. This is a poem exemplifying Aesthetic Realism.

I am neither infant nor happy grandfather
Nor parent, nor lover
Of anyone, of anyone.
I am, as every man is, Majesty,
The North Pole, the Secret, the Stranger,
The will-o'-the-wisp in the distance, the will-o'-the-wisp in the
    distance.

But alas! I cannot remain this way.
I should like to show myself to the world,
So that someone sees me, so that someone sees me.

This is why I sing and I torment myself.
I should love to be loved.
I wish to be of someone, I wish to be of someone.

The First Amendment and the Red, White and Blue

Hurray for the First Amendment,
It's just wonderful.
I love the First Amendment,
I hold it to my heart.
It shows what a country can do,
At a beautiful time.
Three cheers for the First Amendment,
Three cheers for the Red, White and Blue.
For 'tis the First Amendment
That shows what the U.S. can do.
Anybody who doesn't love the First Amendment,
Doesn't love the Red, White and Blue.

Quaint Type and Whirlingness

Watch how now the little crumbs
Of space and time go whirling through
The words of symmetrical lips in the springtime.
And Colonels are among those
Who hear the words and note them down.
Softness is over all; the bells have ceased;
The soft clouds of once have gone; and new clouds come.
We shall have the 18th century once more.
Its soft clouds will come again.
Quiet, commercial towns (that saw many summers)
Will be as they were in any of those summers.
And rhetoric and crumbs as once they were.
And whirlingness will be.
And the drums of softness whir.
And the giant sound of sweet lips
Be the giant sound of now.
There will be no difference.
Every one will note the sameness.
Even the bells will.
Quaint type will tell of us.
We shall die and quaint type will tell of us,
And of whirlingness and time.

Rather Sighed For

A cathedral blowing up,
Two trains smashing,
I look on while I sup,
And wish for a fire also.
Horse going as fast as it can
Through rain and wind on wet road,
And a million airplanes
In a million skies.
Kisses had while going
Many miles a moment,
And crushings of loveliness
Had, going through the air,
Many miles a moment,
With a maddened wind,
And madly curving clouds;
While roofs are leaping,
And oceans rising;
And suns tearing on,
And night changing to day
In a minute,
And day changing back
To night in less;
Often and often.
All this is very pleasant
And is at present
Rather sighed for.

By the Wave

"Write it down,"
Said the wave;
"Look at me."

A Moose Moves

Came then a startling inference
Which moved as a moose moves,
Through the woods, definitely.

For the World

All now there, my God, snow and tears and longings;
Come, God, change; let there be other states, other feelings.
We have died, we have longed, we have borne, we have thought of
    coming things.
And painful snow came when we thought joy would; we are
    yours, O world, come to us as you wish.
Leave your ardors, O world, for our pain; we are tired of sad
    longings, sorrowful hungers, crazy despairs.
Let there be whiteness in our feelings, as there is in your snow,
    O world.
Come, world, let our feelings be other.
Fog, fog is; fog, fog should be no more, fog as we have known fog.
Burn, O world, and kill, O world, and make cold and sad, O
    world, but let there be whiteness in our feelings, O world.
We are yours, O world.
We are, O world, you.
Come, be other, world.

Tree, By Asia, By the Sea

Tree, standing there,
On a heath once,
A heath of short, cold, green grass, pale green.
Tree, the wind goes through you,
And your hard, cold, bare branches shake,
Shake, shake, and the wind goes on,
Goes on till the Atlantic,
Goes on over the Atlantic,
Goes on over the Atlantic, to Asia, to Mexico, to Japan, to Peru,
    to men in Peru, to women in Peru.
For all winds are with each other,
Are with each other,
O tree, standing there,
On the pale green, cold heath,
In Scotland by the sea, near the sea;
All winds are with each other, O cold, bare tree,
Once, once green in Scotland, Scotland by the sea, by the sea and
    Asia, by Asia, by the sea.

83

Something Else Should Die: A Poem with Rhymes

In April 1865
Abraham Lincoln died.
In April 1968
Martin Luther King died.
Their purpose was to have us say, some day:
Injustice died.

Because

Every wayside you see, you have to fall by.
Every thorny bush attracts you.
That's because the self you think you have is not the only one
you have.

Jolly Poster Poem

THE GAY ARTISTES
INVITE YOU
TO AN EVENING OF FUN
AND PHILOSOPHY
(FAVORS FOR ALL)

PROGRAM:

1. Don Hommedieu will explain some New Yorker Jokes.
2. Ev Lanceton will give a short, concise talk on Lippman,
   the Man.
3. Pol Mimmo will deliver an inspirational talk entitled,
   Again The New York Times Points the Way.
4. Dru Winx will render a new dance number called, The Free
   World Saraband.
5. Janx will do card tricks and deliver anti-totalitarian
   Epigrams.
6. Oyster supper, dancing, couples and vigilance will follow.

COME ONE. COME ALL. COME EARLY.
RELAX AND FIND OUT EVERYTHING.

84

Summer Again in New Jersey

New Jersey cops in summer
On New Jersey highways
Have been chosen for something.
You see them, as you may look at clouds
In the midst of July,
With motors about
And the leaves of New Jersey trees.
One can go mad for New Jersey
With its careful selection
Of cops and clouds,
Motors, leaves and trees.
Was there ever a more selecting state?
Just think, it has selected gasoline
To have in it, in summer—
Even though it makes you, or may, kind of sick.
How long will New Jersey go on selecting?
What is New Jersey?

II

Ah, New Jersey motors, you are fine,
You throb in the summer air.
You pass the New Jersey pine,
You go towards Connecticut where
Again, there are cops and gasoline.
Was such an arrangement ever seen
Before? Yes, between Minnesota and Michigan.
Again, gasoline, cops, clouds,
And summer air and summer blue.
Michigan air and blue.
A presence and absence of crowds,
A man walking in summer alone.
The motory summer tone,
The summer of Connecticut.
Reality seems open and shut.
Ah, selecting New Jersey, selecting Connecticut.
Summer Minnesota, summer Michigan.
Summer again.
Summer again.

Every Evening

Every evening had
Eleven men walking
On a leaf-strewn road.

The Lesson of Art

Within debris
Is symmetry.

Hymn, By Charles Baudelaire

To the very dear, to the beautiful one
Who fills my heart with clearness,
To the angel, to the immortal idol,
Hail in immortality!

She is where my life is
Like air tinged with salt,
And in my still desiring soul
Pours the taste of eternity.

Richness always fresh that perfumes
The atmosphere with a dear something,
Forgotten censer which is misty
In secret through the night,

How, love incorruptible,
Tell of you with truth?
Musk grain, that lies, unseen,
At the beginning of my everlastingness!

To the very good, to the very beautiful one
Who is my joy and my health,
To the angel, to the immortal idol,
Hail in immortality!

Murder Is Told Of

Perhaps it was a murder.
Perhaps there had been a struggle.
Perhaps the sun had gone down,
While a man was dying unwillingly,
Being killed by a man he knew.

The curtains were very still
As he came in.
They were rather white.
Outside, the tall tree
Was green and peaceful.

And as he remained in the room,
And later looked out,
He saw a star had come in the sky.
Still he had not done anything
About the dead lawyer
Besides look at him,
And once, touch him.

Then he took a book
About 15th-century England
And read in it a little
About Henry V.
He took other books
And read in them.
And he did not touch again
The dead lawyer, Greening.

He went to bed and slept,
And did not remember much
About what he may have thought of
While he slept.
Perhaps a notion of his boyhood
Came to him.
He thought he had thought
A little about lawyers.

At seven in the morning
He arose

And still the dead lawyer Greening
Was lying there.
It was raining a little
And two people were at the corner
Of the street
On the other side of it.

That morning at ten or so
Landers told the police.
The murderer was never found
And it is now ten years ago.

Seem to Do Most

Thumb on paper
Is something felt.
Thumb and you
Seem to do most of it.

1960 Regret Poems

1. Time, An Indian

Time is an Indian
Knocking off Poskudnaks.

2. Tuesday, November 8, 1960

Next Tuesday, November 8, 1960,
The country will be attacked by two bruisers.
The country will be deceived.
But it will go on.

3. Don't Look, Boys

We got to take it easy.
There seems to be an election.
Don't look, boys.
There is nothing to see.

Kangaroo

God said: I knew
Some day there would be a kangaroo.

Horror Can Use Horror When Ethics Fails

Once Hanoi was not bombed nor was Saigon rocketed.
How has it come that they are?
How does the horror of Hanoi come to be accompanied by a
    horror like it in Saigon?
Does one have to have horror for oneself to realize what horror is
    for another?
Is the only way we can be against horror for another to see it as
    the same as horror for one's very self, for one's self very?
The horror of Hanoi is using the horror of Saigon to tell about
    itself, to inform others, including people far off.
Sometimes horror displaces ethics as a means of telling about ethics.
Horror, like dates, descriptions, diaries, is informative.

II

What did the double horror begin with?
Horror may comment on ethics, but does horror, itself, come from
    insufficient ethics?
Who can have insufficient ethics?

III

Can sufferers have insufficient ethics?
Can the dying have insufficient ethics?
We know the murderous can have insufficient ethics.
We know the powerful and conceited can have insufficient ethics.
We know the ruling and vain can have insufficient ethics.

IV

Horror is calling to horror, using horror to tell of itself.
Let us change it all to ethics.
It was so at the beginning.
Ethics might have annulled horror before one saw it, endured it,
    hated it, feared it.
Ethics can end this horror.
Ethics can end the simultaneous, crossing Hanoi and Saigon horror.

89

Which Fires

This quiet rain, that I knew
Came of divinity too.
Divinity which melts
Divinity which pleases,
Which fires, makes fierily gay.

The Laurels Are Cut Down,
By Théodore de Banville

We go to the woods no more, the laurels are cut down.
Figures of Love in low places, the group of Naiads
See shining again in the sun as cut out crystals,
The silent waters which flowed from where they were.
The laurels are cut down, and the stag, quiet in fear,
Trembles at the sound of the horn; we go no more to the woods,
Where playing children laughed, gathered in abandon—
Among the lilies of silver moistened by the sky's tears.
Here is the grass which is reaped and the laurels which are cut
    down.
We go to the woods no more, the laurels are cut down.

Free Earth

O, Manoona, what shakings of nerves are possible in this many-
    mooned, growing world.
What fallings of a thousand feet and a million; what cutting smiles;
    stopping grins; body hardenings.
A million birds at once; two suns meeting; a growth of a million
    trees; a sky's yellowing; an ocean's leaping.
Mountains growing red; dresses' shocking; flowers speeding towards
    one's face.
Manoona, an allowing world.
Manoona, a free earth.

Roland and the Archbishop: From the
Chanson de Roland

He went then to help Archbishop Turpin.
He unlaced his helmet of gold from his head.
He took his light, white hauberk.
He tore his tunic entirely
And with the bits closed his large wounds.
Last, he held him embraced to his breast.
Then he laid him softly on the green grass.
Roland then asks this of him, gently:
Oh, kind man, grant me this moment, this.
Our companions we held so dear
Are dead; we should not leave them.
I want to look for them and distinguish their bodies;
Carry them and put them before you.
The archbishop answered: Go, and come back.
The field is yours by the grace of God, and mine.
   Roland goes away; he goes alone on the field;
He looks in the valleys, he looks on the mountains.
He finds Gérer and his companion Gérin,
And finds Bérenger and Othon.
He finds Anseïs and Sanson;
And also the old Gérard de Roussillon.
One by one, the baron took them.
He has brought them to the archbishop;
And has placed them in a row at his knees.
The archbishop could not help weeping.
He raises his hand, gives his benediction.
Then he says, Ill fortune has come to you, Lords,
That the God of glory has all your souls
And puts them in paradise among saintly flowers.
Death fills me also with anguished feelings;
I shall never again see the splendid emperor.
   Roland goes away, he again goes across the field.
He has found his companion Oliver.
Against his breast he presses him tightly.
As he may, he comes back towards the archbishop.

Duval Is on the Run: The People Are on the March, By José María Quiroga Pla

Duval sputters at the radio.
(He is to be Jailer-in-Chief when Spain becomes the Jail hoped for
    by the Fascist.)
Duval is talking to his audience of thugs:
"When this war is ended, there will be no prisoners, no wounded,
    and no stones
To tell anything about it."

Duval had thought of everything but the people of Spain!

The people waited for him at Navalperal.
The red flower of Spanish blood waited for him at Navalperal.

Twice the militia of Mangada, our General,
Defeated him; twice set him on the run.

As he runs, he leaves his dead, and his implements of war.
As he runs, he swears filthily: he has learned how in the barracks
    of his officers.

He runs as best he can till he is behind the walls of Ávila.
There his windy braggings are made fun of by the Fascists of
    Navarra.
Duval disbands his column—it was cut to pieces, anyway.
He tilts his triangular hat
And flees on to Valladolid.

He is greeted by an everlasting funeral-chant of clerical guffaws,
Sung to him by the priests of the people—
Priests who went to the fields
And armed in behalf of Spain—
Priests who with crucifixes
Fought their way to the open!
And now the sons of those who are prosperous by the lives of
    others—
Even these timid, sniping, little souls—
Laugh at Duval, slyly, now that he has taken to his heels.

Where can he go? where can the truth be avoided?

For the stones of the Sierras,
And the rivers, heavy in their flowing
With the spent blood of our youth;
And the Spaniards of mountain and crag,
With clenched fists, raised toward the sky—
Are as one in a cry
For a democratic, republican Spain
Born from the depths of our people's being—
And for which now, to give it life, and to save it,
Profusely the people is pouring its blood.

Freedom is comrade to our democracy.
Freedom has taken the form of our militia.
Freedom's arm is raised high.
It carries the proletarian flag.
Sons of the people, let us, as one,
Run after the heels of our would-be jailers.
Let us understand, that, without freedom,
Life isn't worth a spinning cent.
Today we are nothing but—the people of Spain!

There are guns in our hands.
With these we shall hunt
The beasts who oppose us!

The Umpires Are There, With Their Fair and Foul

There was a time when fairness was so much in America, of a
    summer afternoon.
Will it be a fair ball or foul, a fair hit or foul, did he slide to base
    fairly or foully, were questions in American minds, in
    Americans sitting on stone benches, looking: selves where the
    playing was.
All this is of sport—baseball; it is of basketball, football, tennis.
Sport is near to art; it has an ethics like the ethics of the world
    just so.
It was agreeable to think of fair when a blow was given by a
    vigorous someone to a vigorous somebody in boxing.

93

Play the game!—took its place with Kant's Categorical Imperative
and the Quaker Inner Light.
Does fairness include love and war even with these English words
having gone around: the words, All is fair in love and war?
The feeling of man is that all is not fair in love and war: why
otherwise should there be the feeling about extinguished
Lidice and the feeling about the two brothers in Keats' *Isabella?*
What is not included by fairness?
There are two umpires in a big baseball game and they are
supposed to be good about fair and foul.
How would the United States seem now in the eyes of two good
umpires?
Umpires are looking on in the present war doings of our officials.
Foul! is called often and continuously.
It is called sharply and with profound continuity.
Let us see these umpires.
Let us hear them.
Their caps are next to our hearts.
Their voices are our very selves.
Their saying of Foul!—is our blood circulating.
What we are looking for is a sharp hit through the infield, fair
as anything, bounding through all time.

A Sentence of Sir Thomas Browne in Free Verse: A Found Poem

Now since these dead bones
Have already outlasted
The living ones of Methuselah
And in a yard under ground,
And thin walls of clay,
Outworn all the strong and specious buildings above it;
And quietly rested under the drums and tramplings of three
conquests;
What Prince can promise such diuturnity
Unto his Reliques,
Or might not gladly say,
Sic ego componi versus in ossa velim.

[*Urn Burial,* Chapter V]

94

Fine Ethical Moment of Charlie Barnes

Charlie Barnes had a big and true grin.
He said out loud, I know it's a sin
When you see something true and you know it's good,
Not to speak up for it, just as one should.

Charlie Barnes, all clear and all kind;
Charlie Barnes, deep feelings in his mind;
Charlie Barnes rose and said his say—
Charlie Barnes knew it was the only way.

Still the Dawn

Came the dawn
To the man.

Ran the man
From the dawn.

Still the dawn
Waits for man.

Two Stanzas from French Literature about Death: In Stances à Du Perrier, By François de Malherbe

1.

But she was of the world, where the most beautiful things
Have the worst fate.
And a rose, she has lived the life of roses,
The space of a morning.

2.

The poor man in his cabin, with straw overhead,
Is subject to its laws.
And the guard which watches at the entrance of the Louvre
Cannot from death defend Kings.

It and Beauty

A kind of beauty is our quest
Allied to comeliness of insect leaping,
Or of steel by dull pond.
Wars are not against this beauty,
And old hospitals are for its lasting.
Neither volumes nor Cornelia
Can avail against its ability
To whir the nerves and fragments
Within an oblong room.
Ah, this beauty
Is desired, is looked for, is scrutinized.
And all our pockets' contents
And some of our hours' approachers
Are for it,
Are in favor of
It and what it means.

Monologue of a Five-Year-Old

I don't want my father and my mother to get along,
'Cause then I feel I'm not so much.
When they fight, they look at me in such a way,
I know they need me more than yesterday,
When they were nice to each other.
How many things there are I can make fun of.
There's my father who goes to work and fools my mother.
There's my mother who stays at home and fools my father.
Sometimes my father doesn't want to think of my mother at all,
And he does this when he's away,
Though he can do it when he's home, too.
So I make fun of him,
Because he doesn't want my mother to know this.
And then there's my mother.
She thinks my father doesn't know her so much.
(And he doesn't.)
Still, she can act as if
The way my father talks suited her,
Just because she knows he can't do without her.
So I make fun of her.

And when people come to our house,
The way they act that they care for each other
Doesn't seem so much to me, either.
So I make fun of them.
What people say and do,
Is not the same as what they have inside,
Doesn't go with what they have inside.
So I make fun of them.
Maybe I should feel sorry for them.
But when you are sorry for people you may feel bad yourself.
So it's better to make fun,
So it's better to make fun,
And that's what I do,
Inside of me.
And I am five years old.

The Fall of the Leaves,
By Charles Hubert Millevoye

With what was taken from our woods
Autumn strewed the ground;
The grove was without mystery,
The nightingale was voiceless.
Sad and dying, at his beginning,
A youth in sickness, with slow steps,
Once more walked through
The woods dear to his first years.

"Woods that I love, farewell, my life yields.
Your grief has foreshown what will happen to me;
And in each leaf that falls
I read a prediction of death.
Fatal oracle from ancient medical city,
You have told me: 'The leaves of the woods
Will yellow once more before your eyes,
And it is for the last time.
Your youth will fade in lifelessness
Before the grass of the meadow,
Before the vine-branch on the hillside.'
And I die! With its cold breath

A disastrous wind has touched me;
And my winter comes to be
When my spring has hardly gone.
A shrub destroyed in one day,
Some flowers were my ornament;
But my languid growing
Does not leave any fruit.
Fall, fall, frail leaf in shadow!
Let this sad path be hid from eyes,
Conceal from my mother's despair
The place where I shall be tomorrow.
But—the solitary corridor in woods—
If the sorrowing love of mine
Comes to weep here when day has gone—
Make by a light sound
My shade consoled for an instant."

He speaks, goes away—and without return.
The last leaf which falls
Has marked his last day.
They dug his grave under the oak there.
But she whom he loved did not come
To visit the stone in isolation;
And the shepherd of the valley
Troubled—he alone—with the sound of his footsteps,
The silence of the mausoleum.

Note on Circles and Spirals

Circles don't like
To be compared to spirals.
It is unjust to,
Unsettling for, both.

Merriment Can Be an Object of Thought

Reading about any past merriment
Can help to make you merry yourself.
This shows that the past merriment is not over.
The past is never over while it can be thought of.

The Poem of Catullus about Attis

The immediate purpose of this translation of Catullus, Poem 63, is the giving it a clear, English free verse music.

Another purpose is to make clear what is happening, in all its strangeness—so that we can know what we begin with, as we look for value and meaning. Catullus' Latin in this poem is compact, even said to be congested. I have intended, while not thinning or diluting the Latin, to give it, in English, space and poetic, relevant motion. There is a clench often in Latin which, while powerful in itself, needs to be completed by a motion deeply corresponding to the clench.

The oneness of man and woman is adumbrated here with not easily measured power, contriving and unconscious. Since a problem of today is how man and woman can be more like each other, to the luminous advantage of both, the Catullan poem is a mighty, contemporary text.

Implicit, as I see it, in the poem of Catullus is that if one sex is to become more like another sex, it should be to the honor of the sex changed from, not to its lessening. In other words, if a man wants to be more feminine—and this can be right—at that time, he should honor the deep meaning, the inclusive possibility of the masculine. The sexes simply have to honor each other.

Further: if the masculine is feminine, too, maybe it shows we had underestimated the largeness and diversity of what is masculine. Also, if the feminine can be gracefully masculine, it may be that we had underestimated the meaning and possibility of the feminine.

Therefore, this question: Are feminine and masculine, as opposites, deeply and beautifully one in this our world, the way other opposites are?

Taken in a swift bark, over deep waters,
Attis, when eagerly, with rapid foot,
He reached those Phrygian woods
And entered where the goddess was,
Shadowy, this: a forest—
It was there, impelled by madness, by rage,
His mind bewildered,
With sharp flint,
He made fall from him his weight of maleness.
Therefore, when she felt
That the structure of her body
Had manhood no longer—
Even while new blood wet the ground's surface—
With clear white hands
She seized the light timbrel,
The timbrel that is yours, Cybele,

Your mystery, as mother of things.
And making the empty oxhide tremble with her soft fingers,
She began to sing, afraid a little,
Thus to her companions:
"Ye Gallae, let us go, go to the mountain woods of Cybele together,
    together go,
As a wandering number of persons
Belonging to the Lady of Dindymus.
You wished to be exiles, wanted other houses soon.
You were ruled by me as I led, with you following.
You endured the swiftly flowing salt waters, the fierce seas,
And, through utter disgust with love, made yourselves something
    else than men—
Please now the heart of your goddess with your brisk moving about.
Dull slowness put out of your mind.
Go together, come to the house in Phrygia of Cybele;
To the forests in Phrygia of the goddess,
Where is heard the tumult of cymbals,
Where the sound of timbrels is followed by the sound of timbrels,
Where the flute-player, Phrygian, blows a deep instance of sound
    on his curved reed.
It is where the Maenads, ivy on their heads, toss these heads
    violently,
Where yelling shrilly, they toss their heads with energy;
Where that wandering number of persons belonging to the goddess
    like to go, now here, now there;
And to which it is right for us to hasten with lively dance motions."

As soon as Attis,
Woman, yet not truly so,
Said this, in a chant, to her companions,
The lively crowd suddenly, with busy tongues, yell loud,
The light timbrel makes its ringing sound again,
The hollow cymbals clash again.
The rout, with hurrying foot, goes swiftly to green Ida.
Also, Attis, frenzied, breathing hard, unsure,
Their leader, accompanied by the timbrels, wanders
Through the dark forest—
Like a heifer, never tamed,
Running aside from the yoke meant to burden.
The Gallae rapidly follow their leader with his rapid feet,
Until they reach the house of Cybele,
Faint and weary,

After so much labor.
They rest, and they have had no bread.
Sleep, heavy, covers their eyes with weariness, drooping.
The delirious madness that was in their mind
Leaves, in the presence of soft slumber.
But when the sun
With the flashing eyes of his golden face,
Made the now clear heaven light,
The firm lands, too,
And the wild sea;
And drove away the shade night has,
With his renewed eager steeds, tramping,
It was then sleep left Attis, now wakened; sleep was gone.
It was the goddess Pasithea who received him into her tremulous
    bosom.
After soft slumber then, and the being freed from strong madness,
As soon as Attis himself in his heart looked at what he had done,
And saw with clear mind what he had lost,
And where he was,
With mind much in motion,
He ran back to the waves.
There, tears running down from his eyes,
She looked upon the empty seas,
And thus piteously spoke to her country,
In a voice having tears.

"O my country, that gave me life!
O my country that gave me birth—
Whom I leave, being a wretch,
As servants who run away leave their masters.
I have taken my foot to the forests of Ida,
There to live with snows and the frozen hiding places of beasts,
And to visit, in my frenzy, all their hidden living places.
Where then, in what part of the world, do I justly see you to be,
    O my own land?
These eyeballs of mine, unbidden, long to gaze at you, while, for a
    time, my mind is without uncontrol and wildness.
Shall I, taken from my own home, be carried far away into these
    forests?—shall I be away from my country, what I possess, my
    friends, parents?
Shall I be absent from the market, the place for wrestling, the
    racecourse, playground?
Heart, sad heart, again, again, you must tell your sadness.

For what way was there a human could be which I could not be?
For me now to be a woman—I who was a lad, then a youth, a boy,
    the flower of the playground!
I was once the glory of the palaestra;
I knew crowded doorways;
Thresholds were warm for me;
There were flowery garlands for me to adorn my house with when,
    at sunrise, I left my sleeping place.
What shall I now be called?
A maidservant of the gods,
An attendant of Cybele?
Is it for me to be a Maenad, part of myself, a man in barrenness?
I, shall I live in icy, snowy regions of verdant Ida,
Pass my life beneath Phrygian high peaks,
In the company of the hind whose home is the woods,
Along with the boar who goes up and down the forest?
Now, now what I did makes me sorrowful,
Now, now, I wish that it hadn't occurred."

As these words came from lips in rosy redness,
Saying something new to both ears of the gods,
Cybele, loosening the tight yoke of her lions,
And urging on that foe of a crowd of living beings, a foe eager to
    the left,
Spoke in this way:
"Come now," says she, "come, go fiercely, let madness hunt him
    from here, make him, by the coming upon him of madness,
    take himself to the forest again—he who would be too free
    and get away from my rule.
Come, lash in back with your tail, endure your whipping yourselves,
    let all about sound with your high, thick roar, shake your
    bright mane fiercely on your thick neck."
So speaks Cybele in anger, and, with her hand, makes the yoke easy.
The monster enlivens his courage,
Rouses himself to a fury in himself.
He speeds away, he roars.
With foot swiftly covering the ground, he breaks brushwood.
But when he came to where the water stretched from the shore
    gleaming in whiteness,
And saw gentle Attis by the flat spaces of the sea,
He rushed at him.
Attis runs with mad energy into the woods.
He was a handmaid in these woods all his life.

102

Goddess, Cybele, great goddess, lady of Dindymus, let all thy fury
be far from where I am, O my queen.
Let it be others you drive into frenzy, others you drive into
madness.

Ballade Concerning Our Mistake
and Knowledge of It

We're always ready to complain:
Our lives are not what they should be.
We look for sun and we get rain;
And stalking us is misery.
There's something else within our glee,
A touch of sand within our cake.
We hope; and sigh, Ah, to be free.
—But first we must see our mistake.

There are the heights we must attain,
There are the truths we have to see.
There's so much loss, so little gain,
There's surface for profundity.
Ourselves and world do not agree.
We're stubborn, so we do not break;
And there's so much plain misery.
—But first we must see our mistake.

No matter how we hide our pain,
And honor equanimity—
To see ourselves we do not deign,
That is, as an entirety.
We'd rather suffer fuzzily,
And soften sight—the while we quake,
And call for change so bitterly.
—But first we must see our mistake.

ENVOY
And so, dear Prince, when hope seems slain,
And bad things happen, and you ache;
Say this—dear This, against the grain:
But first we must see our mistake.

Towards Homer: Free Verse, Beginning with the First Lines of Pope's Translation of the Odyssey

O Muse, tell of
The man diverse in wisdom,
And much, in his life, with sorrow.
He helped, with his might, to have Troy fall,
Troy with its meaning, Troy seen sadly by destiny.
Her divinely built wall stood no more.
This man wandered from land to land,
Observing as he went from place to place.
The ways of men he noted, how their lives were.
Oh, the seas in tumult that he contested were innumerable.
All, so that, safe with his friends, he come to be on the shore he saw
    first.
The trying of this man was vain.
The god of the sun
Became angry with those men of his who meddled with the herds
    that were the god's.
This god ordained that these not reach
The shore of their first mornings.
O muse of heaven, take some of what happened,
Now lying within fate as record,
And narrate it to our world.

The Voyage, VIII; By Charles Baudelaire

O Death, old captain, it is time! let us lift anchor.
This land tires us, O Death. Let us be under way!
If the sky and the sea are black as ink,
Our hearts, those you know, have rays of light!

Pour us your poison so that it comfort us!
We wish, this fire burns our brain, so much,
To plunge to the bottom of the gulf, Hell or Heaven,
    what does it matter?—
To the bottom of the Unknown, to find Something New!

104

La Salle, As Having You in Mind

When La Salle went down the Mississippi
He might have thought of you, had he known you.
He had lots of time.
As you think of him going down the Mississippi, near Southern
   Illinois, about 1680,
You can think of him, Robert Cavelier, Sieur de La Salle, as having
   you in mind.

The Wolf and the Lamb, By Jean de La Fontaine

The reason of those best able to have their way is always the best:
We now show how this is true.

A lamb was quenching its thirst
In the water of a pure stream.
A fasting wolf came by, looking for something;
He was attracted by hunger to this place.
—What makes you so bold as to meddle with my drinking?
Said this animal, very angry.
You will be punished for your boldness.
—Sir, answered the lamb, let Your Majesty
Not put himself into a rage;
But rather, let him consider
That I am taking a drink of water
In the stream
More than twenty steps below him;
And that, consequently, in no way,
Am I troubling his supply.
—You do trouble it, answered the cruel beast.
And I know you said bad things of me last year.
—How could I do that when I wasn't born,
Answered the lamb; I am still at my mother's breast.
—If it wasn't you, then it was your brother.
—I haven't a brother.—It was then someone close to you;
For you have no sympathy for me,
You, your shepherds and your dogs.
I have been told of this. I have to make things even.
Saying this, into the woods
The wolf carries the lamb, and then eats him
Without any other why or wherefore.

Autumn Song,
By Paul Verlaine

The long sighs
Of the violins
Of autumn
Hurt my heart
With a languor
Of sameness.

All stifling
And pale, when
The hour sounds,
I remember
Days of once
And I weep.

And I let myself go
With the evil wind
Which carries me
Here, beyond,
Like the leaf
Which has died.

Reminiscential Questions

Where now is the mood
Of James Anthony Froude?
Where now is the feeling, unusually jaunty
Of Charlotte Brontë?
Where is that sudden smile
Of Thomas Carlyle?
Where is the gesture, rather blasé,
Of Thomas Babington Macaulay?
And where is the stomach-ache
Of William Blake?
And the mood, so far away,
Of William Makepeace Thackeray?

106

A Strong City Is Our God, By Martin Luther

1. A strong city is our God,
   Good for safety and war.
   With him, we're free of every need
   That our lives have met.
   The old angry enemy
   Deeply means to win.
   Great power and much trickery—
   He frighteningly can use:
   On earth he has no equal.

2. With our own strength nothing can be done,
   We should be quickly lost.
   The Just Man fights for us:
   He was chosen by God himself.
   Do you ask, Who is he?
   He is named Jesus Christ,
   The Lord of Hosts.
   There is no other God:
   He must hold the field.

3. And were the world full of devils
   Wishing to swallow us completely,
   However frightened we might be,
   We should still win out.
   The Prince of this World,
   Whatever grimness he takes on,
   Will do nothing to us.
   There's power; he is doomed.
   A little word can make him fall.

4. That is the way it will be:
   No thanks are needed!
   God's way goes well with us,
   It has his mind and kindness.
   Should they take away our Body,
   Wealth, Honor, Child and Wife,
   Let that be so:
   They have no victory.
   The kingdom he is remains for us.

To the Reader, By Charles Baudelaire

Foolishness, error, sin, niggardliness,
Occupy our minds and work on our bodies,
And we feed our mild remorse,
As beggars nourish their vermin.

Our sins are insistent, our repentings are limp;
We pay ourselves richly for our admissions,
And we gaily go once more on the filthy path
Believing that by cheap fears we shall wash away all our sins.

On the pillow of evil it is Satan Trismegistus
Who soothes a long while our bewitched mind,
And the rich metal of our determination
Is made vapor by that learned chemist.

It is the Devil who holds the reins which make us go!
In repulsive objects we find something charming;
Each day we take one more step towards Hell—
Without being horrified—across darknesses that stink.

Like a beggarly sensualist who kisses and eats
The martyred breast of an ancient strumpet,
We steal where we may a furtive pleasure
Which we handle forcefully like an old orange.

Tight, swarming, like a million worms,
A population of Demons carries on in our brains,
And, when we breathe, Death into our lungs
Goes down, an invisible river, with thick complaints.

If rape, poison, the dagger, arson,
Have not as yet embroidered with their pleasing designs
The recurrent canvas of our pitiable destinies,
It is that our spirit, alas, is not brave enough.

But among the jackals, the panthers, the bitch-hounds,
The apes, the scorpions, the vultures, the serpents,
The monsters screeching, howling, grumbling, creeping,
In the infamous menagerie of our vices,

There is one uglier, wickeder, more shameless!
Although he makes no large gestures nor loud cries
He willingly would make rubbish of the earth
And with a yawn swallow the world;

He is Ennui!—His eye filled with an unwished-for tear,
He dreams of scaffolds while puffing at his hookah.
You know him, reader, this exquisite monster,
—Hypocrite reader,—my likeness,—my brother!

Discouraged People

The discouraged
People were wedged
So closely together in the subway
You could take one discouraged person for the other.

Sameness and Difference in a Tragic Play

The play's about a fight in which there are
Two persons close—but clashing through themselves.
Their hopes are parallel in fear and hate.
Their ways of mind make intersections which
Bring out the horror of the parallels.
Othello, Desdemona meet in love;
But then the world, themselves, are seen in ways
So other, so opposed, a murder comes to be.
Iago is the means of bringing out
The clash within the sameness of the love
Othello, Desdemona say they have—
Announce to father, Venice and themselves.
There's smothering, because what's close
Is also so remote. Othello saw
A certain this, but not a different that.
The *that* inflamed him. Iago saw
The obscure incompleteness of the love—
For evil looks to show its unseen might
By finding vacancy in good. It strikes.

Basho Translations

1. The Splash

Furuike ya
Kawazu tobikomu
Mizu no oto.

Pond, there, still and old!
A frog has jumped from the shore.
The splash can be heard.

2. Her Lunch-Tray

Te mo tsukazu
Hiru no ozen mo
Suberikinu.

Still, not touched at all,
That is how the food was found—
Her lunch-tray removed.

The Voice, By Henri de Régnier

I do not wish anyone to be near my sadness—
Not even your dear step and your loved face,
Nor your indolent hand which caresses with a finger
The lazy ribbon and the closed book.

Leave me. Let my door today remain closed;
Do not open my window to the fresh wind of morning;
My heart today is miserable and sullen
And everything seems to me somber and everything seems vain.

My sadness comes from something further than myself;
It is strange to me and is not of me;
And every man, whether he sings or he laughs or he loves,
In his time hears that which speaks low to him,

And something then stirs and awakens,
Is perturbed, spreads and laments in him,
Because of this dull voice which says in his ear
That the flower of life in its fruit is ashes.

Searing Epistemology; or, The One Thing to Do

Life is a plot to make you think you are alive.
Reality is a plot to make you think you see something.
Yourself is a plot to make you think you are an individual.
Let us enjoy all these plots.

Art Poétique, *By Paul Verlaine*

Of music before everything—
And for this like the Odd more—
Vaguer and more melting in air,
Without anything in it which weighs or arrests.

It must also be that you do not go about
Choosing your words without some carelessness:
Nothing dearer than the greyish song
Where the Wavering and Precise are joined.

Something like beautiful eyes behind veils,
Something like the trembling wide day of noon,
Something like (when made gentle by an autumn sky)
The blue jumble of clear stars!

For we desire Nuance yet more—
Not color, nothing but Nuance!
Oh! only nuance brings
Dream to dream and flute to horn!

Keep away from the murderous Sharp Saying,
Cruel Wit and Impure Laugh,
Which make weep the eyes of Blue Space—
And all that garlic of low cooking.

Take eloquence and wring its neck!
You will do well, in energetic mood,
To use Rhyme made wise somewhat.
If it is not watched, where may it not go?

Oh, who can tell the wrong-doings of Rhyme?
What deaf child or mad black man
Has made for us this penny toy,
That sounds hollow and false heard precisely.

Let music be, more of it and always!
Let your verse be the thing in motion
Which one feels who flees from an altering soul,
Towards other skies to other loves.

Let your verse be the happy occurrence,
Somehow within the restless morning wind,
Which goes about smelling of mint and thyme . . .
And all the rest is literature.

The Idea of Beauty Is Adored in This World, By Joachim du Bellay

If our life is less than a day
In the eternal; if the year now making its rounds
Banishes our days without any hope of their return;
If everything that is born will perish;

What are you thinking of, my imprisoned soul?
Why does the dimness of our day please you;
If, so that you can fly in a clearer place,
You have a well-fashioned wing on your back?

There, is the good all mind desires;
There, the repose that all the world longs for;
There, love is; there, pleasure, too.

There, O my soul, guided to the highest heaven!—
You will be able to recognize the Idea
Of beauty, which I adore in this world.

Ecstasy, By Victor Hugo

I was alone near the waters, in a night of stars.
There was not a cloud in the skies, on the sea no sails.
My eyes went further than the real world.
And the woods, and the mountains, and all nature
Seemed to question, amid confused murmuring,
    The waters of the sea, the fires of the sky.

And the stars of gold, endless legions,
With loud voice, with low voice, with a thousand harmonies,
Said, lowering their crowns of fire;
And the blue waves, which nothing governs nor checks,
Said, bending back the foam of their crests:
    —It is the Lord, it is the Lord God.

Reality Is the Source of the Tedious and, Itself, Is Often Tedious

Reality consists of debris, the outworn, the pale.
Reality is the cliché.
All the thoughts that are useless—"you have to take care of yourself,
    you know"—are sharply of reality.
The mild has depth.
"Appearance isn't everything, but it helps" is of reality straight and
    immeasurable.
The limp is existence.
Ooze in warm October is Things.
The draggingly superfluous began with beginning.
The infinite is squarely and linearly in the next bit of social tedium
    in a county of South Dakota.
Reality has been more inclusive than surmised, for a long time.
Reality is a much more often than a twice told tale not worth the
    telling.
Reality is not worth it.
It is ever so familiar tedium:
Among other things, as it were.

You Can't Miss the Absolute

1.

In every illusion,
There must be something
Which isn't illusion.

2.

Try to see something
Which doesn't correspond
To reality at all—
And see if you can.

3.

If the absolute weren't
Present in your
Latest mistake—it
Wouldn't be
The absolute.

4.

The Thing in Itself
Has a way
Of being somehow
In the latest dimness.
And if you haven't seen it there,
And thousands of others haven't—
It doesn't mind:
It squats.
For the Thing in Itself
Rambles and squats,
And gets into everywhere,
And has been everywhere.
It is in a kitten's mew,
And a waterfall's roar,
And a printing mistake,
And the latest smugness.
Glory be,
The Thing in Itself
Is the least keep-outable thing

Imaginable.
Safe in brain-ganglion,
Safe in love,
Safe in pain,
If there is anything secure,
That's it.
If there is anything accessible,
That's it.
For mystery is the very commonest article
There is.
And mystery is the absolute, otherwise the Thing in Itself,
Present, present, present,
But hinting, Oh, so much.

Femmes Damnées, *By Charles Baudelaire*

In the pale clearness of languishing lamps,
On deep cushions impregnated with odor,
Hippolyta dreamed of the powerful caresses
Which raised the curtain of her youthful candor.

She sought, with an eye troubled by storms,
The sky, already far away, of her naiveté,
Like a traveller who turns his head back
Towards blue horizons crossed in the morning.

The lazy tears of her deadened eyes,
The broken air, the stupor, the sad voluptuousness,
Her conquered arms, discarded like vain weapons—
All served, all adorned her frail beauty.

Extended at her feet, calm and full of joy,
Delphine brooded on her, with eager eyes,
Like an animal who watches over some prey,
Having first marked it with teeth.

Strong beauty on its knees to slight beauty,
Haughty, she sniffed voluptuously
The wine of her triumph, and stretched toward her,
As if to receive a sweet acknowledgment.

She sought in the eye of her pale victim
The mute chant which pleasure sings
And that gratitude, infinite, sublime,
Which emerges from an eyelid like a long sigh.

—"Hippolyta, dear heart, what do you say of these things;
Do you now understand that you should not offer
The sacred destruction of your first roses
To violent breathings which may shatter them?

My kisses are light as those ephemeral things
Which caress, in the evening, large clear lakes,
And those of your lover will dig their tracks
As chariots do or tearing plowshares.

They will go over you like a heavy team
Of horses or of oxen with pitiless shoes.
Hippolyta, O my sister! turn then your face,
You, my soul and my heart, my all, my half of me.

Turn towards me your eyes, full of blue and of stars.
For one of those charming looks, divine balm,
I shall raise the veils of more obscure pleasures,
And I shall have you sleep in a dream without end."

But Hippolyta said then, raising her young head:
—"I am not ungrateful and I do not repent,
My Delphine; I suffer and am disquieted,
As after a nocturnal and terrible eating.

I feel heavy terrors come over me
And black battalions of struggling phantoms,
Who want to lead me on moving roads
That a bleeding horizon closes at all points.

Have we then done some strange thing?
Explain, if you can, my unease and my fear:
I shiver with fear when you say, My angel!
And yet I feel my mouth go towards yours.

Do not look at me so, you, my thought,
You whom I love forever, my chosen sister,

116

Even if you are a prepared ambush
And the beginning of my ruin."

Delphine, shaking her tragic head of hair,
And as if stamping on a tripod of iron—
Her eye fatal, answered with despotic tone:
—"Who then dare speak of hell before love?

Cursed be forever the useless dreamer
Who wished first, in his stupidity,
Taking to himself an insoluble and empty problem,
To mingle propriety with things of love!

He who wishes to unite in a mystic accord
Shade with heat, night with day,
Will never warm his paralytic body
At that red sun which is called love.

Go, if you wish, seek a stupid wooer;
Run to offer a virgin heart to his cruel kisses,
And, full of remorse and horror, and discolored blue,
You will bring to me your shamed breasts;

Here one can please only one master!"
—But the child, giving forth immense sadness,
Suddenly cried: "I feel enlarging in my being
A deepening abyss; this abyss is my heart.

It burns like a volcano, it is deep as emptiness.
Nothing will assuage this moaning monster,
Nor satisfy the thirst of the Fury
Who, torch in hand, burns my heart's very blood.

How our closed curtains separate us from the world,
And how tiredness leads to rest!
I wish to annul myself in your deep throat
And find on your breast the freshness of tombs!"

—Go down, go down, lamentable victims,
Go down the road of eternal hell;
Plunge to the greatest depth of that gulf where all crimes,
Whipped about by a wind which does not come from the sky,

Boil pell-mell with a noise of storm;
Foolish shadows, go to the end of your desires;
You will never satisfy your fury,
And your punishment will be born from your pleasures.

A new brightness will never light your caves;
By the chinks of walls, feverish miasmas
Will creep in, flaming up as lanterns do,
And will penetrate your bodies with their frightening perfumes.

The bitter unfruitfulness of your enjoyment
Incites your thirst and hardens your skin,
And the raging wind of lust
Makes your flesh flap like an old banner.

Far from living folk, wandering, condemned,
Across deserts go as wolves do,
Make your destiny, disordered souls,
And flee the infinite you have within you.

The Oak and the Reed, By Jean de La Fontaine

The oak one day says to the reed:
—You have a good right to blame the nature of things:
A wren for you is a heavy thing to bear.
The slightest wind which is likely
To wrinkle the face of the water
Compels you to bow your head—
While my brow, like Mount Caucasus,
Not satisfied with catching the rays of the sun,
Resists the effort of the tempest.
All for you is north wind, all seems to me soft breeze.
Still, if you had been born in the protection of the foliage
The surrounding of which I cover,
I would defend you from the storm.
But you come to be most often
On the wet edges of the kingdoms of the wind.
Nature seems to me quite unjust to you.
—Your compassion, answered the shrub,

Arises from a kind nature; but leave off this care.
The winds are less fearful to me than to you.
I bend and do not break. You have until now
Against their frightening blows
Stood up without bending your back;
But look out for what can be.—As the reed said these words,
From the edge of the horizon furiously comes to them
The most terrible of the progeny
Which the North has till then contained within it.
The tree holds up well; the reed bends.
The wind doubles its trying;
And does so well that it uproots
That, the head of which was neighbor to the sky,
And the feet of which touched the empire of the dead.

Slanting Soft White on Mountain Is Never Through

One sheep on one mountain;
So it was somewhere a long while ago.
The white of the sheep
Said something closely to the cloud over the mountain, closely.
There was softness in this part of a mountain range.
The sheep was alone, but didn't know it at all.
What kind of sheep it was, the cloud didn't say.
There is so much aloneness that is not known.
Someone is the cloud,
Someone is the mountain,
And the undescribed sheep in slow, ancient white.
Tabriz, Kashgir, Monomana are names which are present now.
Sheep, slightly diagonal, on this mountain
In say, Asian whiteness,
Says something to pistons, teeth meeting teeth, pounding on table.
You have something to say lengthily
And to many things.
White is never through.
Four feet are never through.
Slanting soft white on mountain is never through.

Local Stop, Sheridan Square

I

The subways, as usual, take emotions north and south.
When you are in a subway, emotion goes with you.
Emotion for thousands has come to a stop at Christopher Street,
    which is another name for Sheridan Square—
And the General who rode so greatly,
Is waiting for you in a new form.
There is a little park to the left
That has had emotion enough in it to give new life to Greenland.
But when you come south on the subway and emerge
From rumbling and dark and steps and platform,
The first thing you see is space—
Blessed, hopeful space, in a city as large as any.
Streets converge—Barrow, Grove, Seventh Avenue, Christopher,
But there is space
And that means there is possibility: for space, somewhere, as a
    philosopher might see it, is the same as possibility.

II

When people got out of the Local Stop at Sheridan Square,
There was possibility in the emotion they had.
It was a world seen anew, maybe, or a girl seen as more friendly.
People have come south, all these years, on the Seventh Avenue
    subway,
With possibility as another name for themselves;
And possibility is never wholly unfaithful,
For is it not always possibility?

III

Sheridan Square with its converging streets and space
Is the headquarters of possibility in this land.
It has been that for many persons
Now with homes, resources and thoughts elsewhere than at a local
    stop in Greenwich Village.
The local stop is remembered in towns, colleges, farms, banks,
    libraries, churches, synagogues, rooms:
In the United States as just the United States.

IV

Up those steps at a local stop
People went and there was a new pat in their hearts,
A new looking-for-something in their lives,
And, with all the indications saying otherwise,
That looking-for has not been wholly deceived or disappointed.

V

The space and the streets at this local stop, Sheridan Square, are too
    much like reality itself to play ignoble tricks.
After all, a subway stop in New York City is as much of things as a
    wooded place in Saskatchewan,
Or a level hot area in New Mexico.
And the people who have been within this space and on these streets
Could not lessen its factness as immeasurable in possibility.

VI

Once when you got out of the station, the local stop, of this Sheridan
    Square where streets come together and space says Hello,
There was Hubert's Cafeteria in front of you, if you were looking
    just that way.
Those who once of an evening, of late night—of an afternoon, too,
Were there
Are now in the life of America, in all its regions, divisions, localities,
    districts—in all America.
Some of the Hubert's visitors and lingerers are dead.
(The dead had expectations.)
Hubert's Cafeteria sounds funny, rather low,
But emotion was there,
And spread out wherever spreading could be—
Some of it is now on a ship half-way across the Atlantic—
Some of it is now on a plane three-quarters across the Atlantic.

VII

Births, marriages, deaths have found Sheridan Square indispensable.
And this afternoon—fairly late—many people coming from the
    north will get out here.
They live nearby.
They came from the north once, when they did not live nearby.
They now do.

121

Living nearby in this world, to this world, can be right.
For seeing the world nearby:
Sheridan Square is a mobile, feverish, historical, everlasting, real
and real place to begin with.
It is a local stop.

Hell, Questions, Answers

Hell is a place
Where questions you can hardly hear
Are asked again and again;
And answers, not satisfactory,
Are given to these dim questions
Nearly as often.

Our Leader

I am Your President, a churchman,
And am thoroughly calm
As my bombers burn brown people
(Asians) with napalm.
So retort
To my critics
With your heartfelt
Support.

Boredom Hard to Perceive in Prehistory

If anybody was bored in prehistory,
He would have been remarkable.
It may be, even, he didn't have a name.
To go around without a name
Is already to be so routinish, spacy, other than keen,
You'd find it hard to be bored.
To be enveloped, spacy, rambling, not keen,
Is to be disadvantaged in the matter of perceiving boredom.
Things would lack particularity so much,
Discernment would be so lacking,
Boredom would be ever so hard to notice.

122

THE POEMS LOOKED AT; or, NOTES

Looking at a poem should continue the good feeling or useful perception a poem may have in it. These Lookings, embodied as Notes, it is hoped, in a good way keep the poems going as poems.

Page

3. *Litany of Presidents, Mostly Unfortunate.* 1966. Our Presidents have been single persons. Martin Van Buren was one person. James Knox Polk was one person; it was one person who had so much to do with the Mexican War. Ulysses Simpson Grant was a General and President in singleness. John Fitzgerald Kennedy is in reposeful, regarded oneness. Lyndon Baines Johnson is constructed, seemingly, as one person. Let one be in poetry amidst American history and the singleness of man. (Appeared in *Kauri,* 1967.)

5. *And It Does, Marianne.* 1927. Known persons are one person. But so are unknown persons.—Conrad Aiken once had Senlin tying his tie as the earth whirled successfully and unfelt. I mention this not because *And It Does, Marianne* is like Senlin—it isn't—but because every time I think of Marianne, I think of the Aiken Senlin poem. For the purposes of junction, it may be mentioned that Presidents have sometimes tied their own ties, bow or otherwise. (Appeared in *Today's Japan,* 1959.)

6. *What Now Coheres—Of 1861-1865?* 1959. The Civil War caused many persons to stop dressing themselves before mirrors. How do the years 1861-1865 in America, with their dyings, runnings, and their unknown, cohere? You can use a sonnet to ask a question with. I do this. (Appeared in *Today's Japan,* 1960.)

7. *Necessity and Choice Always Prevail.* 1967. The Civil War had little things in it: most of which are lost. It was necessary in the Civil War, too, to have water stop running when you wanted it to. We now have the water-stopper, grand in simplicity and permutation. It is possible to be equitable with it, quietly.

7. *And There Are New Smiles; New Smiles.* 1927. Smiles took place today that never were before. Let us think of Martin Van Buren smiling. Let us think of Andrew Jackson, "Old Hickory," smiling. Let us think of Julius Caesar smiling: this is strangely useful. Let us think of dead people having some of the new smiles. The poem doesn't mind.

123

8. *Hell, What Is This About, Asked Again.* 1928. Love, with all the photographs of taking women one may see, is still something unknown. And a boy now can ask indignantly, what is that which is in him, making him unable to take his mind off a girl a little younger than he is, maybe. The mystery is there with all the things so plentiful that seem to be not for mystery. The turbulence of reality itself, looking for the quiet it began with, is right now in Taunton, Massachusetts: this turbulence nestles in Jane, looking like a girl in a newspaper—advertising or society section. Free verse can serve this.

9. *A Hundred Plants on an Estate.* 1930. Jane of the previous note has energy. So have the flowers on some estates. Color growing is energy; petals are energy; stems are power. Pink has an overwhelming message both in Jane and in a flower on the estate Harold may see. Along with energy, flowers have number. The way energy and number interchange in the flowers of an estate or garden could make one have respect for the First Cause as botany. The purpose of the poem is to bring about an exuberant, lasting respect for botanical operations and results. (Appeared in *The Literary Review*, 1958.)

10. *And There Prevail.* 1926. The seemliness of petals is in a world having its ancient wars. Not a petal has been noted for itself in Assyria, but chariots of Assyria have been pictured. Holy Writ tells of Assyrian chariots and Assyrian men of combat. Nineveh remains. Edifices may be thought of as burning. Asshur-bani-pal may be thought of as caring for a lily. This last would add something different to Assyria. (Appeared in *Definition*, 1962.)

12. *On American Boys Dying in 1863, in Virginia, and Later Elsewhere.* 1967. Assyria has had wars, and our land has had them too. We don't read much of civil wars in Assyria, but we had a Civil War as great as any. Some Americans, this poem says, must have been wrong at Chancellorsville, for only Americans fought there. This deeply questions the statement: America is fighting—this is all we need to know. How Americans disagreed with Americans in May 1863! The quatrains of the poem cannot conceal this at all.

12. *Musings on Distinguishing an Israeli Cellist from Other People in a World Like This.* 1966. Dead Confederates and dead Union men would look alike after Chancellorsville, for death brings similarity. Every Northern man and every Southern man still, after a hundred years, is what he is, was what he was: will be. A Southern soldier of 1863 like an Israeli cellist is a triumphantly perplexing study in difference and sameness. How an Israeli cellist is different from everyone, everyone who is not that! How indistinguishable, though, he is, seated in a plane with others. The poem is meant to be farcical within the unanswered.

13. *Aurungzebe.* 1931. A baby's cry is noise and can be the most welcome thing one can think of. We don't know of any baby who when born had no disposition to announce its being born, either noisily or soundingly; impellingly or musically. Aurungzebe, Emperor of India, was a baby like this. Mohammed was once a tot. Weeness is in the chronicles. Babyness is in the histories. Short lines can tell of human diminutiveness in the years.

13. *Consider Now.* 1922. As babies announce their new being, Sun, Moon and Earth maintain a quiet and gigantic trio. We can see earth from the point of view of the two other members of the trio. It is possible to be on the sun in one's mind, and contemplate St. Louis. We can place ourselves on the moon, and meditate on the machinery to be found on earth. This means that in the midst of astronomical tremendousness, we may suddenly say to ourselves: And we must keep the earth in mind.

14. *O, Wounded Birds.* 1928. This poem is an early statement of the notion that all reality is the aesthetic oneness of the opposites evil and good—with evil and good not presented symmetrically, but with the evil of one time set off by something not evil of a later time. So rustling of leaves in Ohio is placed with the sound of the battle of Pavia in the early sixteenth century. And a bird wounded at the time of the Pavia battle is placed with a bird of later, joyously singing.—Which is more on the side of reality, evil or good? On which side is time? Reality is complete, and therefore, as Spinoza might say or Leibnitz, favors good. It is hard to think of evil as entire or as entire entirety. Is a dimension of reality completeness —entire entirety? If so, wounded birds are assisted by time, infinity, and all other things. It can be said logically that the oneness of evil as oneness, the completeness of evil as completeness, is in the field of good. Within the completeness of evil as completeness is all the ways evil can be seen— and evil can be seen well. The wounded birds then are in a favoring territory of logic, possibility, and indefinitely good seeing of the undesirable. (Appeared in *Today's Japan,* 1959.)

14. *Zeb Duryea.* 1930. It is possible to take orange, an aspect of the sunset, which in turn is an appearance and possession of earth, and call the world by that color—for the purpose of showing fully Zeb Duryea. Zeb Duryea has indolent orange in his name. Even as trees fall while his arms move, orange is descriptive of the world. It is undeniable that Zeb Duryea has watched moons. The poem also says it is well to see a man in his life seeing wings often, often; and smoke from pipes, undoubtedly.

14. *Leaves Stick on the Coat Collar.* 1929. Diana, as goddess, hunted; and as goddess, created. She was concerned with motion, orderly and sudden; with motion having a seen impact on man, and motion not so per-

ceivably relevant to man. Leaves may go on and stop. Diana went on and ceased. Leaves are of forests; Diana is of forests. Diana was in time, with Zeb Duryea, woodcutter. However this may be, swift leaves are lovely Diana's children.

15. *There Is That in You Which Won't Be Fooled, Johnson; And It Is Liked by the World.* 1966. The world came to Zeb Duryea—of whom few have heard—and it is in Lyndon Baines Johnson, a President of the United States. What was the world doing in this President? First, the world sustained Johnson, for without the world no Texan could live. This is the world as seen. Second, the world asked things of Johnson, for conscience is the world trying to get its rights from a person—as it lodges, in its fashion, in that person. Conscience, the poem says, is displeased but will never give up trying. (Appeared in *Definition,* 1966, and in *Prism International,* 1967.)

18. *Only One Thing.* 1960. We have two kinds of things we object to. One is something we can't see like Destiny, or the-world-as-it-happens-to-us. The other kind of thing we object to is the fact that a piano we want is too large for our quarters, or that a shirt we like is too small at the throat. The second kind of objectionable thing can be called the Antagonistic Tangible (the other is the Universal Intangible). Well, these lines are supposed to be a musical interchange and junction of the two objectionable possibilities in our lives. The delicate throat at last, it appears, complains of something definite: describable. The delicate throat or the person therewith, in other words, complains now not of Only One Thing.

19. *Those Green Dogs.* 1930. Dogs have on one side grass and on the other side people. They tumble among flowers with green stems. A world, with green implicit, with green as possibility and cause, may make for a novel called The Livid Stain. Dogs in a world with green so early in it and so essential, were seen as green dogs, with cause and earliness becoming specific swiftly, lengthily. A world that's green has green dogs—that's all. Even the barking can be usefully seen as green.

19. *Collins and Heroes.* 1932. This poem, somewhat like *Those Green Dogs,* says that since the world was once stillness it might as well have been Collins and heroes. If existence has nothing as a cause, might it not just as well have a little more than nothing?—say, Collins and heroes? Poetry is a good deal about nothing as possibility. This poem is. Further, the resting of stars is made equivalent, in Being, to musing of a little boy. Here we are concerned with the fullness of meaning of anything. Where are thuds in existence? And not only how much do thuds depend on existence, but how much does existence depend on thuds? *Collins and Heroes* is a poem presenting existence as stillness and as abandoned contingency equally.

20. *Beginning with Footfalls about the Northern Dispensary, Greenwich Village: Summer, 2 A.M.* 1966. We leave abandoned contingency, at least somewhat, for a notable, lasting building below Fourteenth Street in New York City. Existence contains what happens in rooms of dwelling houses and hospitals; and I must remember I called it abandoned contingency. What is the relation of emotion and space? How are emotion and space both existence? What place have disorder of consciousness, ailment of body in a century, not so near, not so distant? What has a conscious desire to heal to do with evolution? What is pain in Greenwich Village, 1870?

22. *Cooperating Meadows.* 1961. Confederate Generals were not equally sure of the justice of the Confederate cause. History has often in it men acting as if they were ethically sure, when they weren't. There is evidence of doubt in, say, General James Longstreet (1821-1904). One can see some uncertainty in Lee.—Well, sometimes if a person can say clearly, ringingly, heartily: I was a scalawag. There!—he will be happier. Earth knows. The meadows Confederate Generals roved—these may know. For conscience begins in the touched, seen, walked on world.

22. *Noise Is of All, The World.* 1927. Reality is divided by persons into good and evil, and reality as heard is divided by persons into sound and noise. All sound is noise, for all sound can be seen or heard disrespectfully. Music is the most discriminating, well-arranged noise—so well-arranged the noise is not noticed. And noise, like reality, like evil, is ever so versatile. Earthquakes and dripping are in the field; a groan and a crash are. That noise can indefinitely be seen as sound; and, likely, as music, is the melodious, loud message of churches at their best.

23. *A First in Music.* 1964. Something has been present in music ever since it was hearable: it was the something that made music that, that made sound delightfully respectable, elementally organized. At one time, Martha Baird said what it was, and what she said we have reason to see as true. A musical sound remains what it is, is separate as, just at that time, too, it joins with another sound and the world as such. The particularity of sound is separation; the relation of sound is junction. When, in sound, we hear separation and junction, at once, we, Miss Baird tells us, hear music. Separation and junction are opposites indissociable from other opposites in music like fast and slow, simple and complex, treble and bass, surface and depth, thin and thick, hard and soft, many and one, direct and indirect, assertive and suggestive, intellect and emotion—and so on. On a certain occasion Martha Baird described music straight and clearly as a oneness of opposites. The occasion deserves a poem.

24. *Candor Will Be Mine.* 1933. Can we be more candid than we're interested or than we know? There are two things we find it hard to be

candid about, what concerns us ever so much and what we haven't thought of; have not, perhaps, wanted to think of. We are certain we can be just when we are certain that we should never afflict merry-go-rounds. How are the undiscerned trivial and the crucial in our mind? Candor is the desire to say just what we mean, and is a virtue coming from the insistence of any one thing on being seen wholly as that. Every object, as something to be seen, is multiple in possible virtue. When things are seen as wanting to be all they are and tell all they are—when we see this and are for it, at that time we shall want to be all we are and tell all we mean. "Candor," then, "will be mine." (Appeared in *The Literary Review*, 1958.)

25. *Approaches*. 1958. Asian flowers are thoughtful of American flowers; Asian flowers forgive American flowers in another poem. In *Approaches,* one leaf is thoughtful, in motion, of another leaf. How are things truly to each other? What do roofs think of clouds? What do twigs think of trunks? What does an oak leaf think of a pine tree needle? What does a wide leaf think of a blade of grass? And what do leaves who go toward each other and away, think of each other? The attempt to think about this is already wise. (Appeared in *Today's Japan*, 1959.)

25. *All, All to Be Seen*. 1958. Objectionable people have died. The mortuary has been used to forget where people have been disagreeable. It is fair to all people to say that the people in graves are like the people not in graves. The dead have been sly, curt, insincere, unjust, overbearing, inconsiderate. Bones have been part of injustice, inhumanity, the inaccurate. Everywhere, in death and in life, evil and good maintain their difficult and unfailing relation. Death may be a means of the person called "impossible Susan" actually being better. We must make death as useful and as kind as can be. (Appeared in *Today's Japan*, 1959.)

26. *Boats, Shores, Tides, Fish*. 1965. Ian Hamilton Finlay's *Poor Old Tired Horse* brought forth these thoughts and lines about remaining shores, changing water, wriggling fish. The shore is a study in permanence and circumstance, in the stable and the unlooked for. How boats, shores, tides, fish in their difference speak to each other! They are like leaves to other leaves and like leaves to lawns, like Asian flowers to Iowa dandelions. Difference and sameness can be seen as one through discreet and wise speech. This is so, by a shore of Scotland or elsewhere. (Appeared in *Poor Old Tired Horse*, 1965.)

27. *Bulldog's Hair*. 1930. How intense can relation be? How can space and time be described by what is in them? These are concerns of the poem. An intense relation of other things to bulldog's hair is built up or furthered, while time is seen as described by *attitude* and *grimness* (through *morning*), and space by *wideness* and *flight* (through *spot*).

Through the poem is what a thing is as to the thought about that thing. The thing and thought about a thing are made equivalent. Musings are made as independent in reality as apples. And it is what can be seen in a blurred page of a book that is made equal in all existence to bulldog's hair. And a major dismounting near breakers is made like a major dismounting near breakers told of in a book—and both assisted by *smothering* and *insect*—to lead to bulldog's hair, with *bulldog's* of course leading to *hair*. It is a *leading to* poem, as part of whole relation. If music's there, it helps acquiescence to *leading to* and relation.

27. *This Spring, See the Forgiveness of Asian Flowers.* 1968. America has millions and millions of instances of these subtly and kindly organized rising individualities called flowers. Some are not taken care of, particularly, by persons: these are wildflowers; and some are sedulously taken care of in gardens or elsewhere: these are thought of flowers, near flowers, or something like this. People in the United States have taken care of flowers in the 1960's, and looked at them, gently and responsively; and there has been brutality from conspicuous people in America. Generals and Administrators have thought of themselves in a way unjust to Asians, frighteningly unjust.—What do Asian flowers think of this injustice, this cruelty by the conspicuous? This question belongs to history as poetry, and to poetry when it is history.

28. *Haikus: Some Instances.* 1967. In Seventeen Syllables—Three Lines, with Five, Seven and Five Syllables—the simultaneous opposition and love of things can be usefully told. How a thing one says seems something else when heard from another, is in the first syllable-gathering.—Sunflower and sun meet through a brook.—Something of you begins, in a fashion, as you look at a sunflower.—The best, being accompanied by everything, may now and then be transformed.—Apple, tomato are seen as pedestrians walking in a friendly manner, in a round manner, and in a red manner.—There is a limit on my desire to be seen, but this may change, so come see me anyway.—Since yellow can be seen as honoring green, a whirling banana may truly seem to honor green earth.—So things comment on things in Haikus, or Seventeen Syllables, or Three Lines.

29. *The Print.* 1958. Is ethics within the seeable, the hearable, the smellable, the tastable, the touchable? Ethics has so far been found most in the two "aesthetic" senses—seeing and hearing. The visibly crooked has been likened to evil; the visibly straight to good.—As to the first question in the poem, *The Print,* that has been answered by the speech of man: dark and light have been made the like of wrong and right.—Roundness has been made closer to love than straightness.—And hope has been found in both dimness and clearness—as fear has been found. Man's association of ethics with the visible is either fortuitous, from the top, or essential, sub-

129

stantial, and deep. Is there something in common between how dark is in our minds and wrong is? Are dark and wrong both objects? The way it is seen in the poem is that reality and ethics are both continuous. Wherever there is the real, there is the ethical. The ethical is of reality as much as change, size, motion, shape are. So dark and light as themselves show wrong and right as themselves—the while they reflect each other or are forms of each other: by form I mean here possibility as belonging to something.—This is concerned with good and evil in the print as art; but it should be mentioned that there was a specific print by Chaim Koppelman, *On Meeting Beauty,* which had in it beauty, dark and light, slowness and mobility, all as things the person you may meet next is about. (Appeared in International Graphic Arts Society [I.G.A.S.] catalogue, 1958.)

29. *The Song of the Potter: Ceylon Folk Poem.* 1965. In Ceylon someone once saw pots, likely his own, as having an ethical mission. They had an ethical mission, but they were made amidst ethics, too. Kind grains of earth and wished for drink would be brought by the pots. In this way the goodness of earth would be shown. The pots are seen as discriminating in effect. They are beautiful, what they carry is beautiful, and earth is a cause with beauty. So the potter is delicately praised, too.—This is the source of the poem: *Les Larmes du Cobra: Légendes de Lanka.* Collected by Enid Karunaratné. Translated by Andrée Karpelès. Paris, Bossard, 1925.

30. *Chapped Second Fingers.* 1957. Begin with chapped second fingers in January and be impelled to see better—with the aid of the chapped second fingers—cherry-blossoms later. Relentless January may at least help us prize the ripple in warmth more. Chapped second fingers may assist us better to see green in restrained heat. And we can begin with chapped second fingers to go higher, to branches. All this is so because while chapped second fingers are cold, since they are fingers, our fingers, they are warm likewise. The poem is a making of cold and warmth similar through chapped fingers; also an insulting of cold. Visual and tactual situations are intermediaries. (Appeared in *Today's Japan,* 1959.)

30. *Character Sketch.* 1961. A person is the only being in the Zoological or Divine Kingdom who can be dissatisfied with himself or herself, and know it; and say it. Moreover, the thoroughness or comprehensiveness or keenness with which a person can be dissatisfied with that person's being doesn't have ascertained bounds. A good part of the conversation one has with oneself is darkly critical muttering about self; another good part is less darkly critical muttering about one's foes. The muttering in both fields can be organized. The present poem can be described as First Step in the Organization of the Muttering Against Oneself to Which Selves Are Disposed. People can't help telling themselves how ineffectual they are. Sometimes, like Richard III or Hedda Gabler, they can say how mean they are.

They also can know and say how dismissing, uninterested or contemptuous they are. This poem accents a likelihood man has of telling himself how inept he is; inglorious.

31. *Milwaukee Eagle.* 1926. An eagle in Wisconsin, perhaps near Milwaukee, must have some notion of its surroundings. The eagle perceives something as it flies. It crosses the urban and the rural. It fails to do some things, like "alight on parasols." We can surmise wisely that an eagle prefers clouds to sheet iron. And an eagle is deeply courteous. Furthermore, some things are coming to the eagle. What are they?—Proceeding: the eagle is various. Like man, it can be energetic and tired. People differing among themselves can see an eagle. It has lessons for us. And infinity is as much of an eagle's world as of anything's or anyone's.

32. *1967: The American Past Will Come Later.* 1967 was a low and exacting year for America. What was it doing, or if one wishes, what was being done with it? Wordsworth has some sonnets in which he shows a disposition to be ashamed of England. William Vaughn Moody has his *Ode in a Time of Hesitation*—an Ode critical of these States. One can feel that a country more than three million square miles in area is doing things, or not objecting to things, false to that large country's historical or geographical meaning: false to what the world hopes. The question in this sonnet is whether there is something in the United States themselves, in America itself, stronger in loveliness, in justice as life, than what they or it consented to. The sonnet says the Land is stronger than any unworthy administration. (Appeared in *Definition,* 1967.)

33. *Ode on the Death of a Racketeer.* 1936. The check on free enterprise or laissez faire—as it used to be called—is ethics. Government, supposedly representing ethics, has often restricted free enterprise—for instance, in the field of child labor and "bucket shopping." Yet free enterprise has often been talked of as if the word "free" were clear and virtuous. Free enterprise does go for racketeering or the absence, say, of minimum standards. The freedom of once has been seen later as injustice, as ugliness. Where do the ugliness and injustice of free enterprise begin?—The poem says that free enterprise *must* somewhere have injustice in it, for offhand all that Dutch Schultz was doing was carrying free enterprise to its free-est.— And if "freedom" can be limited, then freedom is not just freedom, but accuracy too. Perhaps then we should change a well-known term to Free-and-Accurate Enterprise; or, perhaps, Free-and-Just Enterprise; or, even, Free-and-Beautiful Enterprise.

33. *The Siamese Tell Us: Let Us Listen.* 1965. The people of Thailand have a right to question some attitudes and doings of the American State Department. As Mr. Pickwick might say, The people of Thailand have not

131

only a right to find State Department attitudes and doings questionable; Sir, it is my hope they find them reprehensible.—And if Mr. Pickwick could see this and say it, it would be well to give Siamese cats an attitude, for they are closer to Thailand than Mr. Pickwick is. In the poem, the Siamese cats we heard are seen as ethical heralds, messengers of right and wrong. Poetry, I think doesn't forbid the seeing of and telling about Siamese cats as announcers, betimes, of international evil.

34. *Rain in Ireland.* 1926. Rain which once fell in Ireland was accompanied by much. For one thing, it was accompanied by England. Ireland, geographically, is fairly gentle, but the Atlantic, near it, is gigantic in spaciousness and might. And as we think of the impressive and variously huge Atlantic, we can think of rain falling on Irish monasteries years ago. Rain fell, fell, not fiercely, on fields cleanly green and yielding. And a girl may be going briskly to her home, a hut. London as usual was near. The Atlantic hasn't changed much. In this comment, I have begun with Rain in Ireland. (Appeared in the *Literary Review* of the *New York Evening Post,* 1926.)

34. *Picketing God, Or Something to Be God.* 1959. We are always asking that if God or the cause of the world or the world itself has good in it we haven't seen, that God show what this good is. Logic was used in favor of a better fate for wounded birds in *O, Wounded Birds.* In picketing God, we summon the logic and kind efficacy of God to show themselves. We ask energetically for an explanation. We ask for an explanation of our own imperfection. We firmly ask for clearness. Wherefore disguises? Impermanence seems insulting. The cause of evil, whatever it may be, must show itself. Our logic can be a quiet picketing. The bounding, impetuous, formed, loud statement of our dissatisfaction with the manifestations and doings of existence is a more direct picketing of God. (Published as a broadside by Definition Press & Terrain Gallery for the Society for Aesthetic Realism, 1959.)

35. *Poem about an Ancient Instrument.* 1966. Some poems are irrefragable, unashamedly convincing. I think this is one.—The major thing is what an ancient instrument and wild grass say to each other. These have been made differently. These take space differently. Yet it is undoubted that a decorous ancient instrument can be placed amid wild grass. The instrument will be what it is to the grass at the very much continuing second the grass will be what it is to the instrument. And while the instrument, in its own way, affects the grass, it stays there. We must rescue the unquestionable.

35. *The Little Cube in Space.* 1953. Our mind can cause things to exist in a useful and legitimate manner.—The mind as imagination can, too, make things exist hurtfully and illegitimately. The Little Cube in Space is

made to exist with subjective accuracy, imaginative propriety. Anywhere in space, the mind can see, construct, and have be a cube of air. A cube of air, or a cube of space, seems more jaunty than air or space which is not a cube. Geometric exactitude, miniature, in space seems dashing, definite, substantial, and lightsome. As we have a little cube exist in space, we have to feel friendly. Here exactitude and subjective fashioning have to be friendly. To have a precise, three dimensional form exist in every-which-way or uncharted space is acting on space and dealing with space amiably. (Appeared in *The Literary Review,* 1958.)

35. *Red and Yellow and Hills.* 1926. Autumn came to American hills unaccompanied by trains. Leaves fell on hills, and hills languidly seemed to welcome the falling. The presence of trains introduced something new to autumn, hills, leaves. Speed arrived and sound—and a rival to the hills as that on which leaves fall, for occasionally leaves fell on trains. The red and yellow of leaves and autumn were not affected at all. And with all the speed and sharp announcing of themselves by the trains, there was much drifting along lazily by leaves. Haze and goings-down of sun, autumnal way, still were. The main thing, then, with all the interruption by trains, was a friendship in color, might, and time of autumn and quiet; of red and yellow and hills.

36. *Invective Against Lake Superior.* 1957. Lake Superior is definitely too indifferent (it is like certain lakes in Asia). Indifference in reality cannot be said to show reality at its best; at its most real. Lake Superior is related to Charles V, but apparently was never thought of by him. (Charles V wasn't able to do much better in relation to Lake Superior. Columbus, it seems, knew nothing of Lake Superior; and Verrazzano apparently didn't: *he* could have told Charles V about it.) One can get angry with Lake Superior, when one thinks of all it doesn't care for. It would be a more useful anger than many angers people have. I believe that poetry asks us to be angry with Lake Superior as a means of being good to all things. What can that mingling of substance and time which I have called "the honeycomb of time," do for Lake Superior? We should ask this. (Appeared in *The North American Review,* 1964.)

36. *Point.* 1928. Our lives come from earth and earth contains them. The earth here is reality still and vivid, reality restrained and having graceful color. Waving pink and merry water question sarcophagi. The question earth asks is, What does it mean for something to be over? And a point on earth can ask this. How is the word *gone* related to reality? Where do perceptions of people go after being had? What do creation and nullity say to each other? Is sadness an insult to cheerfulness, or a completing of cheerfulness? What is the comment of forever on a point of earth?

133

The Poems Looked At

37. *Gaze.* 1930. The growing world can seem sad. Pines have a faculty for seeming sad: they can seem so lonely in greenness and sharpness and a certain kind of incompleteness. That pines don't have leaves—that they have needles—makes pines seem unfinished, unmellow. Some contraction has taken place with pines. Also, to see their sharpness shaping space but not enriching it as a poplar might do, is something to one. Whatever the cause, gazing at pines may begin in sadness, and go on in sadness. The gazing may go on for a long time. The longer the time of gazing the more the sadness seems justified. And after a while, luxury is in the sadness. It is never, though, a snivelling sadness. The sadness that comes to one gazing on pines is noble and accurate.

37. *Running Oxen.* 1930. Everything that occurs in the world makes for another adjective for God or the First Force seen personally. A world in which many hoofs go speedily at once entitles the First Force to be called Hoof-Wielder—as Jove is called Thunderer or Apollo, Far-Darter. And if heads are broken, one can see the cause of all things as the cause of this. And it is the First Force that is present in running oxen and in what may happen to them. The First Cause, or the First Force seen philosophically, can be addressed with rhythmic pomp, with measured and various ceremony, with sincere melodious awe, and with careful pleasantry. It is hoped this happens in the poem, *Running Oxen.*

37. *Condign Punishment for Our Leader.* 1967. There is no doubt that a Chief Executive of America, L. B. Johnson, has had much to do with death. It has seemed to some that he was too unconcerned with the lives of men—with the lives of women—with the lives of daughters and sons. The mortuary prowess of Johnson has been seen as uncalled for by some observers. Perhaps these observers are right; are just. If so, since Johnson has shown a certain satisfaction for himself in attending funerals, he could be obliged by an Evaluating God or a Just First Force to attend the funerals of all the persons whose death needed Johnson's policy to occur by. The attending of funerals consequent on this decision of Supreme Might would take a long time. (Published as a broadside by the Terrain Gallery, 1967.)

38. *September Day.* 1930. Reality can show restfulness, dimness, even fatigue. This can occur in a city on a warm day of September. September, being undecided, may be indolent. But where slowness and dimness are present, one can find hurrying, and a going up of steps. Letitia, the girl in the poem, is like September: with briskness and restraint and dignified, slow softness. Skipping Letitia is in a place growing darker. Food is thought of and worked for in a languid, urban September. Yet there is polished wood—that is on the side of briskness. Briskness and languor everywhere interchange and accompany each other. And through a window, 6 o'clock of a September day, Letitia Barnes may observe a phase of everything, lazy and acting.

38. *At Thermopylae, By Simonides of Ceos.* 1967. The two lines of Simonides of Ceos, translated here, have been translated often. I felt that free verse, casual and falling carefully, might do something useful with the Greek. There is a high, sharp sadness in "O stranger," followed by an inevitable request in the Greek; and this I aim for, in the first line. In the second line there is the lasting submission of "That we lie here," followed by the large pride of "true to their laws." Government and pathos merge delicately and mightily in the second line. And as the Lacedaemonians are told, the telling goes on to and for everyone—for the everyone of now, the person of now. Simonides shows us this is how he saw it; this is how, as poet, he desired it.

39. *Some Lines from Voltaire's Poem on the Disaster at Lisbon.* 1967. Voltaire and Simonides are so different in the poem we are now considering and in the poem before. Simonides sees something so right in Thermopylae: what happened there in 480 B.C. Such historical composure Simonides has; such acceptance of the universe as occurrence. But Voltaire argues. The Lisbon earthquake of 1755 is not something to be resigned to, unquestioning about, says one of the most alert men of all history. Voltaire, though, is poetic too. He doesn't have the brief, undying grandeur of Simonides, but in the lines on Lisbon, Voltaire shows he is poetic Voltaire. Grace, music, largeness, surprise, wit—and, again, auditory loveliness are in the Lisbon lines. Voltaire and Simonides have both complied with the Muses' pleasing monitions.

40. *Stillness in the Field.* 1924. Summer and winter are alike through lilies and snow: there is stillness in the field. Lilies can do something similar to what snow does: present geography and existence as unheard. The days bring another kind of stillness to the stillness that has left. There is a procession, ever so modest, of otherness and continuity. The sun, as before, has clouds with it. The hours are as correct as ever in their change. The hours, however, have a one by one motion-quality different from the way lilies are there and snow moves and falls. Distinction must be recognized in the way things, physical and otherwise, quietly seek kinship.

41. *This Is Your Cup of Tea.* 1965. Pottery containing the flowing is a fairly good instance of the reality of Parmenides and the reality of Heraclitus joining forces. It took a long while for pottery to become a cup, with that cup sedately and consummately welcoming and containing tea. Tea doesn't seem to belong to anthropology at all: it is too distinguished. Were a cup to contain water or blood, we should be more in the prehistoric— though a cup argues against the prehistoric. With all that's unknown in history or prehistory, whenever there is tea in a cup, a wild, quiet force— the flowing tea—is disciplined and enclosed by the decorously imperious cup. And opposites, as the poem says, are everywhere, just existing at

once: like each other, for they serve something which has them both, in the way a plane always, always has shape or outline and width or mass. A cup of tea emulates the world in being severity and flexibility at once— the tea can be considered as flexible. God, as something needing opposites for his work, shows his method in a cup of tea. (Appeared in *Poor Old Tired Horse,* 1967.)

42. *The Cydnus, By José Maria de Heredia.* 1950. The sonnets in *Les Trophées* of José Maria de Heredia can be regarded quite properly as four-teen-line cups melodiously and definitely containing their historical tea. Heredia had his fourteen-line form and then looked for something in history (or it might be just in landscape, with history faint) to become words, lines, sentences, rhymes, rhythm, so that an abstract form, tried in literature, bob, remain, and be various with verbal flesh. (Keats and Words-worth did something like this in English, but not with the stylistic, melodious, undeviating rigor of Heredia.) Heredia is sonnets and hardly anything else. History and love at the edge of Asia Minor are in this sonnet. A high sun is stopped by a trireme, which in turn is contained by river's flow. There is the delicacy of incense as rowers work hard. Flutes and silk are in motion.—Cleopatra is given the severity of a seeking bird. A soldier's quiet face awaits the seeking, mighty bird. And as queen and soldier look for each other, intently, there is a whirl of the abstract so much in life: desire, death. The whirl has its reposeful place in the sonnet.

42. *The Greatest Chinese Name in the World.* 1950. It happens that two English monosyllables, so expressive of the hoping and affirming individual, sound like an example of Chinese nomenclature. We are in the world and we add something to the world, and if existence is noticed, we want to be, too. We all say to the world in our manner, You are; and we all say in our manner, if You Look or One Looks, one will see Me Too. There is no narrowness, conceit, exclusiveness in saying everything can see Me Too as I can, given the chance, see everything. Me Too is a great Chinese name. There is none greater, perhaps. You Are is as great. (Appeared in *Poor Old Tired Horse,* 1965.)

43. *Heaven for the Landlord; or, Forthwith Understands.* 1959. Land-lords would like to feel virtuous or justified as they go after a mighty thing in the economic structure, Rent; as they go after Increase of Rent. Every-one who feels virtuous feels Heaven is on his side; and so Landlords must feel that Rent and the Increase of Rent are favored by Heaven. And if Heaven favors these, the structure of Heaven must be in accord. Earthly obduracies and obstructions attending the Institution and Increase of Rent would therefore not be at all. Tenants would be thoroughly educated in Heaven. Heaven as Landlords see Heaven is no place at all for exaspera-tion to property owners arising from controversy as to the monetary return

one gets because one has consented that someone use or live on the property one owns. Obvious, but some people have not thought of it. (Appeared in *Definition,* 1963.)

43. *The Milkmaid and the Pot of Milk, By Jean de La Fontaine.* 1949. Jean de La Fontaine is a good narrator, as he chooses the taking and musical word. The way he has the milkmaid become a property owner (somewhat like the Landlord in the preceding poem) is some of the charm of the seventeenth century in France. There is soliloquy in the poem, marked by events. The French girl's mind has animals in it: there are useful animals in the girl's mind as she walks. She argues with herself and wins, all within true French poetry. The catastrophe is within true French poetry, likewise.

44. *They Look at Us.* 1968. Martin Luther King on the conservative side is with the slain Abraham Lincoln. But as one who went out in the streets, he is with the non-treatise-writing John Brown. It is easy to think of John Brown, like a star, looking down on us, seeing how we shall do. (Vachel Lindsay has a good poem on the subject.) And we can now think of Martin Luther King, too—in the company of John Brown—looking down at us, observing. Shelley says something of the kind in the last lines of *Adonais:*

> I am borne darkly, fearfully, afar;
> Whilst, burning through the inmost veil of Heaven,
> The soul of Adonais, like a star,
> Beacons from the abode where the Eternal are.

From this, we can see John Keats with Abraham Lincoln and Martin Luther King: there is no reason we should not. Indeed, every star can be regarded as the largest meaning of a person: for a star looks. To look down from on high at us is to be in the employ of a world careful that what it, the world, is, be loved as much as is deserved.—And John Brown, too, wanted some way of looking at the world loved rather than an acquiring way of particular parties.

45. *Happiness, By Arthur Rimbaud.* 1958. It is good to have Rimbaud tell us that the going after happiness is as inevitable for a person as being affected by gravity is for a solid object. The light and the heavy are in seasons and castles, time and edifices. And Rimbaud tells us happiness is a magic study, but we have to give ourselves to it.—As a cock in France crows, you can hail energy in any living being concerned with happiness. Something in us can, irritatingly to self, use self-importance against happiness; but this is a burden. Self-importance can seem to be a charm, but it scatters the energy of self and body.—Again, we must put together the non-weighing seasons and the weighing castles—though both seasons and

137

castles have shape of a kind.—When one definitely goes away from happiness—the hour of flight—death will be yielded to.—Therefore, again, O seasons—O time as visible; and O castles—O weight as white and distant.

45. *The Town Called Sleep.* 1959. The question about death is whether it has its place in Evolution or Universal and Particular Improvement. It is quite clear that when a person dies, he does improve in a way, for he doesn't make the same mistakes any more; he can't—though a legal will may remain, powerful in injustice and mischief. Will personalities get the chance to be as complete as can be, true to themselves as can be? Is Existence a Stopping Personality Arrangement or an Improving Personality Arrangement? One cannot say for certain that it is just the first. The possibilities of reality—not easily measurable or limitable—cannot be said to exclude more self-development than is patent. The unseen is a factual aspect of reality: the unseen or unknown is that, but it is just as factual as the seen and known. The universe simply consists of what we've seen and what we haven't; what makes sense for us and what doesn't. The relation of fact and making sense is a somewhat new subject. Nothing in reality is not busy. One way for reality to be busy is to have The Town Called Sleep—because one of the names of reality is Possibility; and one of the names of Possibility is Sensible Imagination. Three roosters have not likely been for four hours at a Stringed Instrument Concert, three days in a row. But it could happen one of these three days, if we thought it would do any good. (Appeared in *Definition,* 1961.)

46. *The Whale.* 1922. The whale has gone about its business these centuries, even when pursued. It has had, or whales have had the same hours and days we have had. Life for the whale is, seemingly, beginning, process, end. These three—beginning, process, end—don't leave anything out, except as both Kierkegaard and Aristotle might say, God or Existence or Reality itself. And the whale shows reality, so it shows at least an immortal thing: what we are represents, at least, something immortal, infinite. The opposites in us as one are equivalent to immortality or infinity, and the whale has these; as the fly does. The way reality—and any reality at its beginning—is constituted is immortal. The pattern for reality is reality unstopping. So the whale in its lumbering fashion represents or instances something unceasing in reality. As the whale stands for reality, it is particularly the whale: what, however, is within particularity says something of existence as nothing and something: that is, as always.

46. *There Is the Vivacious John Randle of Doylestown, Pennsylvania, 1817: A Found Poem.* 1967. I felt a rhythm, mixed with winsome descriptiveness, in this advertisement printed by a Pennsylvania newspaper in 1817. The advertisement was made known to me through Tom Shields who came on an offset facsimile of the journal as he acted in Bucks County of the state mentioned. Time and offset married.—Liquor, GREEN TREE,

Randle, Woodruff meet; and then after FEED, we meet TAILORING BUSINESS. Certainly enough is met in the first Presidential year of James Monroe. The important thing, however, is the gentlemanly, honest melody in the lines latent in the advertisement. Occasionally, latency made manifest, is resplendent in subdued harmony. I think that's so here.

47. *The Story of the French Revolution.* 1959. The past like the present consists much of change from no to yes, nothing to something, and from less of to more of. Once there was no Julius Caesar, and then there was. This means that the nothing aspect of Julius Caesar gave way somewhat to the something aspect of Julius Caesar. And Julius Caesar as less of was displaced by Julius Caesar as more of. Change has always been of kind and degree in an ingratiating and deep way. For example, when Caesar died, we cannot say of this, there was no Julius Caesar: for clearly, Caesar occupies us. He has an effect, and has had it for long.—Once, as historians tell us, there were signs of the French Revolution—these have been found in the thirteenth century. But there was no French Revolution. Then there was. It is good for poetry to give a big historical event a birth like that of a heard infant. Suddenness is in history, including the sociological part. The French Revolution was born as French children were born; also English; also American. James Fenimore Cooper, massive and imaginative novelist, was born in the year of the Bastille's taking.

47. *The Resolution of Conflict in Self Is Like the Making One of Opposites in Art.—Eli Siegel, 1941: Its First Form in a Chinese Manuscript, Circa, 250 B.C.* 1966. If there is a central objection to Tao—and I believe there is—it is Tao's making a crashingly and tinglingly multifarious world too unified, too manageable. This can be seen as a general objection to Eastern philosophy: the philosophy doesn't take account of every hansom cab in the London of 1884. The Lovely is too often the Grandiose. The Surprising is too often the Conceptual. Some Monism—of the West, too— is wearyingly Monistic. We get tired of Unity and want a little Awkward Shattering. We yearn for the Uncouth Fragment. Negative and Affirmative just can't help being the same in certain manifestations of Tao. The Way covers everything as Lake Erie includes all the shipping on it. Spinoza and Kant, I believe, suffer also from the incomplete presence of aromatic, unmistakable particularity. And I'm afraid Hegel does, too, in a sizable number of paragraphs. At this moment I insist on making the Way equivalent to the livest counter eating-place America can have: a counter-place warm, friendly, definite in cold weather; helping the Food and the Way: cold weather which is a most amiable and sharp opposite to the warmth in the room with a counter. And I like seeing the Way in warm tugboats amid ice somewhat.

48. *This Seen Now.* 1927. The subjective is two things: it is, as self, completely occupied with what it is and does; and then, because it goes after

139

being truly completely occupied, becomes interested in something else than self. A subjective fly would be interested in some quick motion towards it—who knows, maybe a desired slap as the mind of another has it. Self-preservation makes for an intermittent extension of objective awareness in everything. Meantime, the unusual extent of the fly's objective apprising is in behalf of its subjective security. A lady crossing a street has something of the subjective-objective arrangement a fly has in coping with a more than usually difficult flatness. It is good to think of vital Subjectivity occasionally having to hail the Objective. The objective then is used to affirm the dimensions and possibilities of the subjective. Through it all, lady and fly see the world and themselves with some similarity.

48. *These Are Five Haikus.* 1967. The Haikus say: Reality in all its fearsomeness can bring us closer to what we're hoping for.—Daisies persist a little and the shadows attending a daisy today may be like those attending the daisies yesterday. In their manner, shadows persist, too.—A ceiling can be seen as being where it is through the bidding of a spoon.—Grass and river have the same strengthening message to the sky.—White tile can be like a hazardous plane for a cockroach to cross. Cockroaches have hazards. I am glad I had the cockroach do well, or likely do well, with the hazard in Haiku 5.

49. *To Dwight D. Eisenhower, with the Presence of Hart Crane and Antonin Artaud.* 1966. To find Dwight D. Eisenhower ridiculous is not, I think, being unjust to him. The profound is something pretended to in Eisenhower. Because of the grimness of his appearance, and the deliberation of his speech, and because of his position, a human weightiness and depth have been given to Eisenhower which are deserved just as well by thousands of townsfolk. And Eisenhower is not generous. There is something mean in him. Love for human lives as such is not his. The stolid emptiness of the General, the stodgy vacancy of the Executive can be given freshness by the addition of rather bold metaphor. So Hart Crane and Antonin Artaud are employed to describe human absence, character infelicity. In the first lines, the profundity Eisenhower has been endowed with is compared to a False Lady of the Sorrows given to a nave of an unfinished church by giant rooks (that is, not such good people) who earlier had taken away an architrave. False intimations of profundity—wrinklings and corrugations—have gone deep into the Eisenhower attitude or character—or "ethos." Ignorance becomes somewhat specific in Eisenhower—the "mediaeval" becomes "Romanesque" in a manner making for new evil. The victory of more culture over less culture at Leuctra, 371 B.C., that is, the victory of the Thebans under Epaminondas over Sparta, has been hurt by Eisenhower—he has spread desolation in Leuctra. Culture and the truly delicate—a small river—despise Eisenhower. That which disdains what Eisenhower stands for—the backs—have the peaceful presence of God in it or them. If Eisenhower is not complex and profound, let the way he is

disparaged employ Hart Crane and Artaud, so that at least the way of disparagement be complex and profound.

49. *While Two Shots in Spring.* 1927. Killings in Wyoming have been accompanied by quietness. Two men shoot at each other; one falls. The other goes off. The grass seems to be in accord. Spring doesn't seem interrupted. Sun and animals are quiet. Consequences there were, certainly—but consequences amid immediate acceptance. Bullets have acted as if they were accustomed to the meaning of this. Quiet went before and quiet went after two shots, active, at the same moment in spring. And we can be sure the world will, in coming days, assimilate what occurred. It is like one large stroke of a bell in an otherwise hushed day. It is like one clap of thunder in a soundless week. The poem is a study in the relation of sound, soundlessness, consequence.

50. *Wove.* 1960. An object is given assertive, unnamed existence through assonance. A woven thing is woven of something, and to say this in four accented syllables is to point unquestionably to the material woven. There is a this; but the *this* is surmise, not name. And the material of the woven thing and the process of weaving are in the sound-clash of *of* and *wove*. Noun and verb are different in these two lines—the noun is what was used, the verb is the using. And it is about time that noun and verb should quarrel through assonance: noun and verb quarrel even though the syllables in assonance are first a preposition and second a past participle. The quarrel within things taken for granted should be told of.

50. *Rhymed Couplet.* 1927. Rhymes accent the sameness of words, but there is sameness among all words. Far away, there is rhyme in the sound of all words. You can find a little rhyme in *machine* and *calm*; *division* and *dove*; *hectic* and *pellucid*. Can you find rhyme in *trellis-work* and *shoes*? As we see it, the answer is yes. Occasionally a rhyme—perceived in obviousness—brings two disparate or warring notions together: as *oak* and *poke*; *debris* and *glee*; *trice* and *ice*; *nor* and *adore*.—So, if differing notions, clashing things, can be brought together through rhyme, might we not expect that words apparently not rhyming have the effect of rhyming because they (one) fall in a line in a similar way; (two) assist one word or are related to one word: the word here is *dew*; and (three) have one informative function, tell of one result? This is why *trellis-work* and *shoes* rhyme for the spirit.

50. *This* The Egoist *Will Do: A Found Poem,* 1967. *The Egoist,* a severely avant-garde journal of the years of the First World War—a journal in which James Joyce, H. D., and Marianne Moore appeared—once had a discriminatingly bumptious advertisement in *Poetry* of Chicago—in February, 1918. The discrimination of the advertisement and its bumptiousness helped to make for, I believe, a funny rhythm, which, while funny

141

is the rhythm of poetry. (The advertisement had in it a better poem than most that appeared in the basic columns of the journal.) When *The Egoist* talks of its desire to present those efforts "which ultimately will constitute 20th century literature," it is somewhat like Pistol with his "Have we not Hiren here?" As *The Egoist* goes on praising itself, making its distinction undoubted and extensive, we are in the midst of the cerebral and the academic and also the bombastically and subtly complacent. (Well, in the third third of the twentieth century, *The Egoist* doesn't seem as good as it said.) Surprising, surprising is the use of "virile" in the last part of the advertisement—*The Egoist* will do only for "virile readers"; and one might think it was a journal for big game hunters, mountain explorers, and motor-boat managers. The ad is funny as the timeless is in it, and as culture and cerebration as uncouth are in it, likewise.

51. *This Is History*. 1926. The existence of history as a true study depends on whether the past is a fact—with the completeness of other facts. History is the just description of the past as reality; and a just description of any reality has all the beauty and all the exactitude of that reality as one thing. The wars of the time of Newton belong to history; his meditations in his garden or room also belong to history. As in art, a slight thing may become important through how it is seen, its relation, its representation of the permanent and large. Well, roses have affected much the mind of man; therefore, what occurs with or to rose petals is in history. The falling of rose petals in night stands for a big thing in the life of man: Leaving. That a rose petal should leave a rose is like Charles V when he abdicated as Emperor of the Holy Roman Empire. Is the cause of a rose petal's leaving in night important? Does it show evil gracefully and gently; somewhat sweetly?—And a ship may welcome, or come to, heavy, dark waters as a rose petal leaves and falls. Motions as form are centrally in the past. The description of the past is history. Motions as form, then, are in history; are history.

52. *Helicopter Explains*. 1965. How can aircraft used not justly be proud of itself? In the poem, a particularly ethical helicopter tells about itself. It did not like the way it was used—if this is not possible, the world is poorer. This particular helicopter wanted cessation of the way it was used, with the least trouble or hurt. What else could it do then, but fall of its own accord, discreetly? Perhaps we allot to inanimate things less ethical discrimination than, now and then, they have. The inanimate is in an ethical world; a world one great part, phase, quality, substance of which is value, or ethics. A helicopter may come to be affected by ethics or value in a manner hard to transmit. As Montaigne, however, might say, Who knows all about helicopters? Yea, who knows all about himself?

52. *The Expiation: I; By Victor Hugo*. 1966. The humility of Napoleon as he retreats from Russia in 1812 is told of by Hugo with the accompani-

ment of cold terror, variously. What Napoleon liked least—confusion—is now his lavishly. Hugo was, it is said, excessively ready to hail Dieu, Temps, Mort, Espace, Moi, but here he is detailed enough. He is like Balzac with a rhythm not Balzac's. Dream and the separate articles of war are in the poem. Atonement and uncertain men in snow are in the poem. Loneliness accompanies a big thing in history. An army is lost. Napoleon is insulted; but he is dignified in his unexpected humility. It is not, though, the final punishment. That, as Hugo sees it, is the being followed by a relative of his, Napoleon III, as ruler of France. What Napoleon did not see is the largest tribulation and lessening. The way Hugo describes and evaluates makes you inclined to believe him. It is not, with all the terror, cold, death, retreat, the one Expiation of all.

54. *The Stars That Summer.* 1958. The history of the world contains things that are steady and unsteady. If stars are considered as of the history of the world—and there's not much reason that they shouldn't be—they belong with the steady things. Abstract things like size, change, cause, or consecutiveness, dimension, content, impact, meaning are the steadiest things as such: the more abstract a thing is the more steady it is. However, stars are quite high in the field of steadiness: how much steadier they are than election and income. And steady things like unsteady things have two kinds of effect: direct or physical effect and through meaning. If stars had an effect on our climate the way the sun does, or as some people say, directly on the fates of individuals, then stars would take their place with wars, steam, electricity and such. Still, it must be said that the way the stars seem to have an effect is through meaning: a meaning not wholly unlike that of art. There the stars are, summer after summer, waiting to be seen, to be thought about, to be distantly beneficent. (Appeared in *Definition*, 1964.)

54. *We Have Had with Us This Sun.* 1927. Every sun has been just in the way it has given light. Its inclusion of beds in early morning has been just. The dreariness accompanying a morning sun has been fairly apportioned. People have conducted themselves differently in early morning, but the sun went about its business with no disproportion.—At 7:10 A.M., in some November, the sun was there, working fairly with beds. The sun's relation with sleep is accurate, though people have been uncomfortable. Mists change and people do, but the sun is just. The persons the sun does things to have names, many names. The sun I am talking of, we have had. Its history has not been completely told. Yet it is good to say, We have had with us this sun.

55. *To a Slushy Pear.* 1966. A slushy pear is one of the many things instancing the carelessness and shape of existence. (I could have used a wet shirt, also, to present reality as sloppy and shaped; or a book on which rain has fallen.) A slushy pear, however, tells of existence, abandoned and

143

formed in a way only it can. Certain functions of the slushy pear are unparalleled in a world of resemblance. To be noticed about the slushy pear now present is its radiance, its effulgent, spotty brown. The sun worked within the slushy pear—just as the poem says. And a slushy pear has the pear contour—notable in horticulture and botanical sculpture—notable in visual recurrence and possibility. The slushy pear has land as a cause—the way other kinds of pears have and boulders have. Sadness is in the slushy pear, for it looks so undecided. Compared to other growing or grown things, its look is shiftless. The slushy pear is one of the few things that, clearly, can be called transitional. A slushy pear and a long stay are not about the same thing. Transition is of the very being of the slushy pear; in the universe, transition is always to be discerned, but as something findable in something else, not something itself. The slushy pear seems to announce: I am transition.

56. *A Lady, Sun and Rain.* 1925. A lady once living in a quiet street of a rather large city looked at the sun after rain, and didn't see either sun or rain as close. She saw conditions in her home as having more to do with her self. This lady's self was exclusive; the lady's self was inclined to diminish most things. There were many things to which she didn't give the meaning they required. Her way both of liking what she saw and giving meaning to it was hardly what it should be. Though this lady's life was in reality, she saw reality too much as an interference, not enough as material for self-increase, self-evoking. She did not see—though beautiful herself—what was beautiful as a means for the very freedom and fullness of herself. She was pretty herself, but the way she saw reality was not exceedingly pretty.

56. *L. B. Johnson Should Be Given All Time to Understand the Pain He Has Caused.* 1968. Life, it has been felt, is too short to understand itself; a person's life is too short for that person to understand where he has been, what he has been, what he has felt, what he has done. This is true of the least crowded life. But the life of L. B. Johnson, President, 1963 and afterward, has been crowded with pain and death, with lives coming to an end, perhaps unjustly. Our Leader simply has to understand why so many people died. Does he have the time? Does he have the time to be equal, in mind, to the pain he has caused? And how long a time must he have to comprehend the injustice he has permitted? It is beautiful to think of Johnson's understanding what wrong he has done, what injury he has let be. Johnson needs lots and lots of time to understand the evil he has liked. The poem says that it is likely our Chief Executive needs immortality to understand all he needs to understand, all he should see otherwise. Let, for this fine objective, immortality be.

57. *Address to Death Acknowledging Its Full Presence.* 1927. The Death that our Chief Executive has encouraged is a diverse mystery, swift in the

unrealized. The geography of death is amazing in scope: one of the places death illustrates is Kentucky. Death can affect an orange dress in Kentucky. And death is not absent from where glass tubes are; it can rise higher than any branch. Death has joined other frequent realities in Kentucky. Death can be compared to white, to fast waves, and to confusion at two: the result is praiseworthy. In some way, death is superior to just misery and to dust coming from shelves to the outside. We cannot be sure as to how much Death is responsive to our thoughts. In the same way that we don't know wholly what reality is, or any reality, so we don't know what Death as reality is. The logical construction of the situation is this: If Death is a reality, then it has things in common with all reality; if Death is not a reality, then we should talk of it that way—which we don't. The relation of death to all things, including the inanimate, should be considered. The relation of the reality of death to the reality of berries, spigots, type, crests, ripples, horns, tightness of lips, running, tiredness, gongs, impacts should be considered. How it came to be in Kentucky amid so many other things, should not be forgot—at least as a question.

57. *Anonymous Anthropology.* 1961. There were men for many, many years before there is one person with a name, whose hand we might shake and whose opinion we might doubt. Anthropology, or the science which deals with men trying through centuries to be men as most frequently thought of, simply lacks personalities. In the Bible there are dim personalities like Nimrod, Enoch, Jubal, but it is worse in anthropology. All the personalities are dim, ever so dim; indeed, there are none. Paleolithic man, Neolithic man must have had individuals who chose to lie down on the grass, lean on a rock, or wander by a body of water; but this is not how men of the Old Stone Age or the New Stone Age have come to us: they come to us all at once, with no names, no individual dispositions, no birth marks, no secret hopes, no particular manner of expression, no psychical apartness, blaze or suggestion. This, so far, is the way of anthropology. Anthropology lacks the unique more than a desert does, or a flat, immense table. If, scientifically, we could change this, it likely would be gratifying. So far, anthropology has submerged the bizarrerie, charm, impact of individual psychology. Anthropology is so collective in its psychology, you can forget it is psychology at all. At this moment, hope seems to be busy again.

58. *Frankie and Johnny, Changed by a Malign Spirit into Dorry and Johnnie, with Words on Aesthetic Realism, the Opposites, the Terrain Gallery, Purpose B and the Hope of Man.* 1960. Dorry and Johnnie stand for two writers on art who made for just wrath because of their slyness and lack of courage and their unfairness about Aesthetic Realism. It is good to give a great American tune to these two. There is reason to feel that while not liking each other, they joined in the desire to hurt or destroy the seeing of art as the oneness of opposites. It is felt that Dorry and Johnnie

145

were not wise as to themselves in their low fear of Aesthetic Realism and their low desire to hurt it. One of these later days, what is true here will be seen. These days, we have two editorial persons' hate and bad ethics told of as if they were two persons of the 1870's in America, fortunate in a great melody and in a lovely, rough, loping stanza.

59. *Through Winds.* 1926. As families and persons went west in the last years of the eighteenth century and in the nineteenth century, trees made sounds. The trees had their own concerns and their way of expression, as a child with difficulty went through woods in autumn. The winds made trees mournful as the journey in behalf of settlement went on. Trees cried as children fidgeted: this is part of the inhabiting of the American West. And trees cry now, cry with the journeying and settlement over. But the little child did go through Kentucky, through Missouri, to Oregon. The child went through autumn and those winds which made trees cry. This is something good, it may be surmised, for the trees. Life can traverse the winds which make trees cry. (Appeared in *The Literary Review,* 1958.)

59. *Mourn This Sparrow, By Gaius Valerius Catullus.* 1967. Here again is the renowned sparrow of the first century B.C. in Roman territory. Is there a more famous bird in the age that is ancient? This sparrow and free verse can be friends. Free verse can have import and casualness the way a sparrow can: free verse should have this. The death of this sparrow is an occurrence lingering wherever lingering can be; the death, in a fashion, is more immortal than life sometimes hopes to be. The harshness of Orcus will not die. A cause is given for the eyes of a girl being red and heavy with weeping, and that cause persists in saying: I'm here.

60. *My Ranch: A Composition by Our Leader, Lyndon Baines Johnson.* 1965. It is likely that history will see the first Texan Chief Executive of the United States as complacent. L. B. Johnson like most people is satisfied with himself in the wrong way; his complacency is grievous. The ranch possessed by the Chief Executive has, it is likely, been used to foster and justify a misplaced complacency—an unfortunate complacency. Quiet and acres may be used to approve of an erring ego. L. B. Johnson has wanted things to agree with him, and there was his ranch ready to oblige. Our Chief Executive, though ill-doing, has the notion that he is misunderstood: this has happened before. A ranch can "butter" an unkind self-structure. A ranch can be used as a cooperation with dishonesty. It is likely that L. B. Johnson would not be authentic without a ranch, but the ranch he has, we are sorry to say, sustains what is least desirable and most hurtful, approves of what is most unauthentic, least genuine in the continuous justifier of the Vietnam War.—In the poem Our Leader is seen as expressing that decided approval of self encouraged by his ranch.

61. *Cue from Cuba.* 1960. It is possible that there are some Cubans now on their wide island who are happier than their grandfathers were, or grandaunts—or other people living on the island say, in 1907. Cuba had unhappiness, we are told, long before its present rule. All the Caribbean islands, Mexico, and Central America, all of South America, have this in common with Asia Minor: they would like to be happier as places and people. Puns are used in this poem, some of them impetuous, graceless, and determined, to indicate that something about happiness may be learned from Cuba—the "cue from Cuba." The names of Latin American countries can be heard in two ways: one as themselves, and the other as English and saying something in the field of historical ethics, or related to the field of historical ethics. And so there is ethical sport with Costa Rica. Syllabic gaiety is found in Colombia and syllabic wisdom in Chile. Guatemala has in it a monition; so has Panama. Peru can be made a verb, with choice in it. Venezuela can be heard as a useful verb. Bolivia can be made a verb with aspiration. Orotund, almost religious verbs can be made of El Salvador and Ecuador. Honduras interestingly sounds like *endure*. Argentina can be made a noun standing for something desired. Both Brazil and bacillus sound like "be silly." And the fact that *guy* can be heard in both Paraguay and Uruguay—or made to be heard—is employable. Mexico can be a verb and Dominican Republic a verb phrase. Puerto Rico can become a wise, opulent adjective. Haiti and *hate* sound so alike, maybe I shouldn't mention it. And Nicaragua can be a noun standing for just outcome.—Well, so all this was seen.

62. *Earth, 1920.* 1920. This poem is the earliest of the poems in *Hail, American Development.* It was written in 1920 when more than ever in the history of the world, one part of the world was calling another dark. The poem has a good deal to do with how Russia in Asia and Europe was seen by other countries of the world and how Russia saw them. Where was the insufficient light? Earth, before, had been various in ethics, culture, knowingness of industry, certainty of government. In the poem, Earth is looking at herself and she knows, at least, where darkness is in her and where light is. Quite permissibly she is made to be tearful as she sees herself in a glass, and sees where dark is. She has seen insufficient light for many years. What should Earth think of herself? What did Earth think of herself in 1920? What did the indispensable mirror of Earth tell? We may not know. Earth may have known better; and may know better this very day.

62. *Hymn to Jazz and the Like.* 1966. By now it is felt that Jazz has added something new to the world seen as art. Further, it is felt that Jazz is continuous with Virgil, with Villon, with Piero della Francesca, with Berlioz, with Shelley, with Swinburne, with Ibsen, with Delacroix, with Yeats. Jazz is a new junction of the deep and the lightsome, the permanent and the unexpected, the continuous and the surprising. One aspect of jazz,

Rock and Roll, points to the heavy and light or mobile as something in Jazz. Jazz does that which Mozart did not have the time to do, but which is in the Mozart field. *Waiting for the Robert E. Lee* is not wholly absent from Rossini territory. *Hold that Tiger* resembles a particularly intense, abandoned, even forgetful chant of the seventh century. The way *Onward, Christian Soldiers* begins is like, to me, the early loudness, rush, assertiveness of some Jazz.—Therefore, in seemly manner, this Hymn to Jazz; for Jazz has hovered over the hymn so long, it should, at this time, have a Hymn to it.

64. *Death's Intention and Opposition Thereto, 1861*. 1959. The Rappahannock, Virginia river, is emotion-laden; and will be. Spring 1861 by the Rappahannock can be looked at without end. Young men on horses with green leaves above them are immortal and sad in perception of any time. Death and the wisdom of a leaf were close in Spring 1861 by an old Virginia river, named once by Indians.—The wise leaf of the last couplet stands for the wisdom that perhaps one can see in reality, the explaining and pleasing something in reality. An episode is surrounded, accompanied before and later, by time, space, meaning: these intensify and assist. (Appeared in *Today's Japan*, 1960.)

64. *Fare Thee Well*. 1966. As Antony asked and said, looking at the dead body of Caesar:

> O mighty *Caesar!* Dost thou lye so lowe?
> Are all thy Conquests, Glories, Triumphes, Spoiles,
> Shrunke to this little Measure? Fare thee well—

so one could ask in 1966 whether all American history had culminated in a narrow, unkind, military management and spoilage of some Asian land. —Were selfish administrators to supersede Bradford and Jane Addams? Was Rusk to seem mightier than Whitman and Boone?—There are signs that America may be herself again. There were signs, strong signs, that she wasn't herself in 1966.—We have to say to America as Antony said to Caesar, and of Caesar: Fare thee well.

64. *I Am So Glad I Am Not Fulton Lewis Jr.'s Niece*. 1966. A particularly reprehensible person in the History of the Expression of Opinion in America is Fulton Lewis Jr. Mr. Lewis had an inclination and an ability to make sociological evil sound reasonable and what was more just to man and America sound incorrect, not preferable. Mr. Lewis was ardent and industrious in behalf of debilitating dark. So one can be glad not to be his niece, even though one finds in oneself, as girl, what one doesn't like. The girl in the poem unabashedly tells of the unlikable done by her and in her —but, thanks be, she is not a niece of the person who used the air and

148

the press to keep America backward, unhappy, unseeing. Is this girl's method of consoling herself valid? It is not entirely valid, but it is a good beginning; and for the field of thought it includes, it is reasonable.

65. *In a Painting*. 1956. Painting follows the imagination, and is a willing servant of it. You can imagine the Brooklyn Bridge rising and looking far out on Long Island or somewhere else—and painting would go along with your seeing Brooklyn Bridge "stand on its hind legs," as someone might say. You can put a little eye in a white cube of sugar. You can take an iron bar and have it, while in the ground, change, somewhere near its top, into a flower like the flower next to it. This means you have given a flower an iron bar for its stem. Painting would accommodate you and your imagination.—In the poem, imagination and painting do the very desirable thing of twisting toast. A scheme of existence, or a frame of being, in which toast in no way can be twisted would be not all that is needed. Twisting toast in a painting shows that a universe always can be more than it seems.

66. *Carry Me Away, By Henri Michaux*. 1968. The desire of a person to be anywhere else, as long as it is else, is strongly in this poem of Henri Michaux. The details chosen by Michaux are disparate enough and close enough—surprising enough and coherent enough. One can be within a Portuguese boat and also in the distance—in a caravel and in foam and in the stem of a caravel. One can be carried away into another time, into snow, into dogs' breath, into a collection of leaves. One can be transported into kisses; one can be placed within breasts; one can be of palms and smiles; a person can be placed within corridors of long bones, and within corridors of articulations. Where can one not be carried? Where can one not be "dug deep"? The Michaux poem is irregular, while it exemplifies one of the most recurrent and one of the most human ideas.

66. *Come, Spring Flowers*. 1924. When one's wish is the same as what the universe is doing, we should know it and be glad about it. The universe and one's heart can coincide in intent, be alike in direction. This can be seen in the well known American adjuration, Shine on, harvest moon. Often we feel like telling earth to do what, of itself, apparently, it is doing. Most dawns have not been objected to. Ameliorations in the weather have been quietly applauded.—All this is relevant to the short poem, *Come, Spring Flowers*. The entire world can be seen as engaged in the having spring flowers come once more, but we can hail the work; and go along with it, too, by discreet verbal encouragement. Spring flowers are usually seen as in our way in the good sense of these words: English, changeable language, has another sense. The annual presentation of themselves by spring flowers is destiny, time, history as an amiable trio; amiable to one-self, oneself. (Appeared in *Today's Japan*, 1959.)

149

66. *Gluck Found Unidentified Flying Objects and You Can Hear Them in his* Orfeo. 1966. All music was once the world of Unidentified Sound, or Unarrived at Auditory Propriety and Surprise. The music we have is a snatching by man of instances from the Unmeasured Territory of Sound as Variously Right. (The contrary of music is sound with no internal scheme whatsoever.) Gluck in the eighteenth century looked for What Sound Had for Him, Comely. A composer selects as he listens, affirms as he explores. For a composer to write down what he hears, descries, affirms, selects is to make choice Unidentified Flying Objects into something else—something, maybe, that others will identify for years. And so, music is talked of, Gluck is talked of, with a beginning in a frequent phrase of our day, concerned with, it is said, visitors from a far elsewhere. (Appeared in *The North American Review,* 1967.)

67. *Humanity.* 1961. The weakness in humanity seems inseparable from it. The worry of Arthur about the next day seems so characteristic of him. And Barbara's lack of principle doesn't seem incidental. If Cornelia is forgotten—and she is—the being forgotten seems something essential about her. The nonblending desires of Dave are of Dave deeply.—It is hard to see what he desires in the fears of Edward.—At this time we should ask, How much do we see the weakness of a person as being that person?—What about Frank, smooth and stopped?—How much is the unseen fear of Gertrude her very self?—Picture now the only possibly listening Hulbert.—Is it the true Ingrid who says mean things?—Jacqueline may be confused, but she's adroit about it: is *the* Jacqueline present here?—Laziness and ambition abide in the entity that is Kenneth.—Has Louis a center?—Is Manny's attitude to money of the center of Manny?—Nona dislikes people and is in delicate health; Ottfried is of long ago; Paul's mind can change without his knowing it: do we have three true people here? Quincy, Rachel, Sidney, Thomas—four people of our time—exemplify humanity as unimmaculate.—Ursula is double, Viola is dim, Winnie is frivolous, Ximena doesn't exist, Yolanda coughs purposefully—what does all this say of the human structure?—Zoë is wrongly passionate, and as we consider her, we have to ask: How is humanity, the presence of the responded-to world in a single person, already off to an awry start?

68. *Decision: A Wildflower.* 1957. It is easy to get the fact that reality is both wild and controlled into a few words. Reality at this moment is showing itself this way: for this moment itself seems so unplanned and so necessary, in the same evening perception. A wildflower grows as it will, but as it grows one can say rather truthfully that where it grows is where, everything considered, it had to grow. And our decision is a wildflower. Should we decide to write a letter to someone, and should we do that, the decision can seem a fact with insistence; but it came from some lazy everythingness and seems to have risen in a territory having habit too: the field of habit. It is all so spontaneous and Necessarian. If after this one doesn't see that decision grows in our field as a wildflower grows in a visible field, the usual field, we'll have to abide this. With it all, it may be said that decision can be wild and wildness can instance decision. Reality is sequence and anything, this year, too. (Appeared in *Today's Japan*, 1959.)

68. *July Room*. 1933. The seeing of the moon from a July room by old men stands for the desire one has to be just to permanence in change. Chandeliers are things down here, giving multiplicity to the moon, and trembling partiality. Moreover, those aware of the moon may often have bent down to look at daffodils. We have, then, upward oneness and lower sweet fragmentariness, for daffodils may seem fragmentary presentations of earth. The seeing man may give himself more to a daffodil than to the hand of a titled blonde. The moon merging with the chandeliers of a July room is the world as entire and lasting and the world as broken up and detailed. One can never be tired of seeing how the absolute—the moon in the sky—merges with chandeliers and July room—the relative as down here. Absolute and relative are an inexhaustible show in their mingling and difference.

68. *A Need by Philosophy, A Passage of Kant, In Lines: A Found Poem.* 1959. In the poem, *July Room,* the moon as absolute merges with the more relative chandeliers of a July room. How something unseen, how something "above the sphere of all possible experience" is yet so effective as "to extend the range of our judgments" is a theme as central as any in Kant's *Critique of Pure Reason.* The distant moon can be among July chandeliers; something unseen may be present in everyday thought. Kant is poetically passionate about this as the introduction to Section III of the *Critique* begins. He should be passionate; it is well that he is poetic, at least *in posse.* For how what is undying, true about all existence, or the whole world—put more dully, how the *à priori* is present in thought as such, or as customary—this question is the world as poetry. Immanuel Kant in his *Critique* says that to reason is to use and be instigated by the structure of the world in the human mind. The *à priori,* the world as our unconscious, the cause of thought in us, is not experience in the customary sense: it is that enabling experience.—Well, it is something to be poetic about. And the lines of Kant have a ring, a diversity, an energetic flowingness distinctive of the poetic.

69. *She Is Waiting, Dear Hippolita.* 1958. Hippolita can be seen as the objectionable in us and outside of us. Hippolita can be seen as the weakest thing in ourselves waiting to take over, or she can be seen as a girl in a different city—just as unlikable as something in ourselves. Hippolita stands for restlessness arising from disapproval of oneself. Hippolita stands for sloppy self-condemnation regardless of what is good in ourselves and the good of other people. She will not take criticism or silence—as something

in ourselves won't. She stands for the disbelief in ourselves as praiseworthy, for if we are truly worthy of praise in any fashion, maybe the world in which we are, and without which we could not be, is worthy of some praise, too. This dreary girl, being, or inward abstraction is formidable; but she likes your company better than her own, for her name on high is Dreariness as Victory.

70. *Logic, Roses and Red.* 1927. Roses say something, with logic, about the world. The roses say, If we are red, the world, source of red, is red, too. And if sunsets are red, and if Indians might be red, the cause of the world is, a little, working in these as it is in roses. The way the world as cause is in roses is of logic, exceedingly of logic. Whatever cause is, it shows logic in every aspect of itself as cause. Cause and logic have this in common: they are about what has to be. Cause is what has to be first, for something else to be; logic is what has to be in how cause works—otherwise, as the skeptic says, it is not cause, just antecedent. The poem says that there must have been the cause of roses in the world; that the world was a world having not only red implicit in it, but the red that roses have implicit in it. Furthermore, that how the world having red implicit in it came to make and have roses with red, is of logic; for cause that works without logic—what philosophers like Leibnitz called sufficiency—is not cause but something else. It is good to think of red inseparable from logic, cause and roses. It makes the world as abstract and as sharply and richly visual a continuing world. If we see logic as beginning with how the world does things, the likeness of logic and beauty can be apprehended. In everything that the world does, one can see logic and casualness working as one, or logic and illogic working as one: and to see logic and illogic working as one, logic and the casual as one, logic and freedom as one, is to see what's beautiful.

70. *Payment for Honesty: or, A Family How Impelled?* 1964. Since Aesthetic Realism has been insulted, not looked at, neglected and attacked for the purpose of killing it, it could be expected that persons thought of as friendly to Aesthetic Realism be dealt with carelessly and brutally. The Koppelmans were, in the article mentioned in the prefatory quotation. The Koppelmans were talked of and written of with unfeelingness and slyness elsewhere.—The unkindness shown to Aesthetic Realism and the Koppelmans as friends to it is quite documented. The sharpest unkindness perhaps is the not asking by Press and Radio why the Koppelmans—and others—were so interested in Aesthetic Realism and talked of it the way they did. The lack of inquiry was like the absence of rain for growing things. The cold, complacent, wide brutality to Aesthetic Realism will some day make all people rub their eyes; and the way the Koppelmans were talked of and, occasionally, talked to will make all people wonder in startling, precise horror. The poem tells about this. The poem is true.

71. *The Waving of the Grain.* 1961. This summer grain will wave again
—much of it tall—in the United States. However beautiful wheat, corn,
barley are, they are commodities. The sun is concerned with them, but so
is the Stock Exchange or a Board of Trade. Labor and machinery are con-
cerned also with the proud grain, bending and rising at various heights
in United States fields. The western United States has most of the tallest
grain: acres, miles, many of them, have grain, waving, dominant in them.
Grain prevails in millions of square feet of western land beyond the Missis-
sippi. The economics and the beauty are inseparable there. These should
be in the best possible junction with each other and indivisibility about
each other.

72. *Impassioned Lines Comprising a Tribute to the Historic Meaning of
Bernard Goldfine.* 1958. The good deed of Bernard Goldfine of Boston,.
man of finance and business, may now be somewhat forgot, but it should
not be. Sherman Adams, advisor to President Dwight D. Eisenhower, took
on a quality of New England incorruptibility; the appearance of a pa-
triotically frugal person like John Quincy Adams; the likeness of a more
than usually simple and strong personality in one of the dull poems set
in New England, of Robert Frost. It was, however, ethical incompleteness
by the White Mountains that Sherman Adams had, and, later, showed. The
way to judge a person is still how much he cares for the good and strength
of all people; for the increase in beauty—that is, kindness and accuracy—
of the universe. Sherman Adams was imperfect here. That Bernard Gold-
fine, with all his frailties, uncommendableness, helped to make this clear,
makes America, in its ethical capacity and role, always indebted to B. Gold-
fine.

72. *Lovely Little Fisher Lad.* 1926. *Lovely Little Fisher Lad* is an ex-
ploration—thorough—of melody, silliness, and sadness. The simple ballad
rhythm with quietly mingling consonants and vowels is gone for; the
rhythm, I believe, makes for a presentation of sadness in uncertainty.
Vowels and consonants can assert and then draw back: I think that is
what happens in the first stanza. The little fisher lad is supposed to be
diminutive and winsome—not alive at all points; and so he is silly. The
littleness of the fisher lad is intended to be unachievingly irrelevant to
earth as gigantic and significant. Still, the little fisher lad is there, in all
his not measuring up. And, with his littleness, he is seen as a source of
paining indecision—is he entitled to this? Does Delftware have a right to
be a major concern? Should porcelain permeate one?—These questions
hint of melodious silliness—with melody existing, mattering.

73. *Intactus; or, Nothing Doing.* 1965. The poem, *Invictus,* of W. E.
Henley is a good poem—perhaps his one unquestionable poem. Despite
the poem's goodness, it has been used to place ego in a bad relation with

what is not it: that is, the external world with all its unlooked for, not likable behavior. There is no limit to how much we can find earth, world, universe unsatisfactory—reality *has* to be infinite in unsatisfactoriness. But ego or self can likewise be inefficient in felicity, beauty, act. *Intactus* is a poem asking that we be fair in the criticism of what is not ourself and what is. The world is unkind—but we may have gall. The universe is harsh— but we may not want to learn. The world causes fear—but our desire not to know it is a desire with contempt for the world often in it.—And our method of protecting ourselves from the world, asserting our apartness, may not be so handsome.—Well, this supplement to Henley's poem, or this Something Else seemed necessary.

73. *Disclaimer of Prejudice.* 1965. Among the many things one may have a prejudice about is a city. (People are the most likely material for prejudice.) Whether it's because Chicago has notable stockyards, or whether it's because it is not by the Atlantic Ocean but is inland, or whether it's because Chicago is not as old as New York or Baltimore, the present annotator is aware of an unwillingness to give Chicago all possibility of goodness and handsomeness: the present annotator, then, has a prejudice. Were this prejudice likely to damage the order of things much, or be a foe to justice, it wouldn't be manifested so willingly. Just because the prejudice is not narrow or noxious, it may be right to call the poem Disclaimer of Prejudice—that is, Disclaimer of Mean, Hidden Prejudice. Maybe, though, the title is all wrong. The purpose of the poem is to have prejudice and a brass band on a June afternoon close. When prejudice is outrageous and not concealed in the least, it should be looked on as something else. The prejudice about Chicago is free and large: if the explanation is labored, it may mean that one should disclaim prejudice and stop right there. The poem, beginning again, is, as will be seen, a disclaimer of any *but* municipal prejudice. Once more, a stop.

74. *A Woeful Ballad on Faking Away.* 1959. The previous poem is an elaborate attempt to disclaim ordinary prejudice while exulting in what may be a special kind. Even so, there may be obliquity or falsity in the poem. However this may be, falsity beckons successfully to nearly everyone and is always beckoning in some manner. Falsity has in the history of mind been more attractive, commodious, rewarding than the truthful. The sea of ego is sailed on by comforting, unsubstantial craft. There is a fear of meaning something utterly or wholly in the population. We like to have a secret interpretation along with the one we give audibly. Timidity and complacency are both causes of our faking away with what we feel. Strategy thrives on our being able to be dual, to be part of a double narrative, or, if one wishes, have a double narrative part of us. Evil can be propounded and presented metrically, with the syllabic effect associated with poetry. This is done in the lines carefully entitled *A Woeful Ballad on Faking Away*. May it be pointed out that Faking Away is opposed by a

term from the Greek, appropriate for both Rhetoric and Theology? The term is Plerophory, which is a distinguished word for Full Conviction.

74. *General Westmoreland Wants Glory and Isn't Getting It: A Military Soliloquy.* 1968. General William Westmoreland, commander of the United States armed forces in Vietnam, is ridiculous in everlasting mournfulness. It is hard to think of a general with a cause that was worse—an American general, anyway. It takes some time for history to be clear about the limitations of generals, and, in the case of William Westmoreland, the limitations are more than usual and more askew. The Vietnam war was a war that some people determined was right, without believing it. General Westmoreland was caught up in an ominous, unsurpassed wave of military and acquisitive insincerity. The relations of the American army to the Saigon officials will one of these days make for reading cruel and bizarre. Only if Westmoreland had no feeling at all—and I feel he has some—could he have felt he fitted into it all. Westmoreland like nearly everybody else was a dutiful misfit, an obedient false note. Westmoreland was a mighty false note. His essential discomfort is, it is supposed, in the soliloquy. The Westmoreland position was funny, with mournfulness surrounding the funny, and beneath it: a great, unendurable mournfulness, later to be studied truly in American history.

75. *Matter Moves on the Avenue.* 1926. Bodies can be thought of without clothes; clothes can be thought of without bodies. Clothes can seem principal. Clothes can be thought of as the main thing as persons go up an avenue. It is convenient to think of a person walking up an avenue as being three things: a body, a self, clothes. As we look at a person walking in a city, it is hard to distinguish between body and self, but when we see that body and self clothe each other, that body can be seen as the garment of self, and self as the unseen garment of body—what self does this body have? is a question with sense—we are ready to see clothes as clothing body and self engagingly. As clothes march by themselves on an avenue, body and self are put in a new relation.—Well, the purpose of the poem is: One, to have clothes by themselves determinedly marching; Two, to have body, self, clothes simultaneous realities, saying something useful to each other. If body is not in the clothes which march, body has that likeness to nothing which self in its immeasurable importance has had for years. Where is self, and if you know where self is, what is it? What distinguishes it from nothing as position, possibility, summary?

76. *Sunlight in Slush, in Puddles, and in Wet Municipal Surfaces; or, Miracle on Eighth Avenue below Fourteenth Street.* 1966. Man has been called rightly a reflecting being because his mind does something with what comes to it. Man is the most gorgeous exemplification of the subjective-objective mystery and everyday occurrence; for he looks at something, the

something comes to his mind and stays there, and the object that was once outside of his mind now is something a man can look at in his mind—say a stream in Wisconsin or a scuffle in Seattle. When we consider a stream in Wisconsin we once saw, the object is in the subject: that is, ourselves. This is reality high class.—Reflection in our minds begins with something like reflection in water; and later, in mirrors. You can see a tree in the water it is near and hangs over. But you can also see the sun not just in lucid water but in dark water; and it is a sun not near to water, the way a tree is, but far off. Also the sun is repeated: it visits every pool of dark February water. Shiningness is in low murk. Since self is a reflecting thing, reflecting everything it is concerned with, a pool of water by a New York hardware store is the self in an early state when this pool of water contains the definitely effulgent sun. By this, hope not hopelessness is advocated. This is the partiality of the poem.

77. *Spark.* 1958. We live by each other, and this means that sometimes when we are inert, a lively thing from someone else combats our inertia. Anyone can say that the spark or livingness in one has an inclination to grow fainter, less bright, or slower. At this time, the spark of another may be doing well; so it is merely wise for us to replenish our agogness through the unlessened agogness of another. Moods are not simultaneous: we may be sinking while another may be rising, with a desire to tell all about it: with a desire, benevolent though not wholly seen, to change our sluggishness into liveliness. Sparks are in the field of altruism and difference. We should know what can bring valuable motion to us. Therefore, it is well to ask: What is your name, bystander?—A person who observes us may have a good effect on us. And it is good to ask the question: What is your name, wayfarer? For a person whom we observe, though he may not be sure of himself, may have a good effect on us. There is that in us—the spark —looking for something not in us—a spark, too. This looking for a spark may have all the wistfulness and distance of the world: this is why the last two lines of the poem have yearningness, surprise, immediacy in them— or should have.

78. *Putting on a Glove Did Something for You, Anyway.* 1953. The being able, gracefully, to put on a glove is, this poem says, something strengthening for a woman. A woman, like everyone else, needs to be assured in a world not lavish with assurance. That we can wear something that goes with us, covers us with trim appropriateness, makes us think better of ourselves. Clothes show, or can show, the exterior world may assist us. The hand of a woman stands for what she is, keenly; for what she may mean and do. And if she can show to others she has a friend adapted to her hand as herself, she is disposed to feel strengthened. A deep, aiding thing is hers when a glove trimly enfolds, contains feminine fingers. Certainly, the glove—as the poem says—cannot do everything. But how its proper junction with a girl can bring a delicate, poised haughtiness to the girl. And

protection without just a little haughtiness may seem incomplete.—The phrase, "fits like a glove," likely has more in it than thus far is seen.

78. *The Albatross, By Charles Baudelaire.* 1967. Baudelaire wrote some ingenious moral poems—which have in them Lamartine, Sully-Prudhomme, Francis Jammes, let alone William Cullen Bryant. *The Albatross* is one of these ingenious moral poems. It belongs to the Ethical Bestiary of the nineteenth century. The albatross becomes part of an anecdote; the infelicity a poet may be near is before us—and the infelicity is striking, sad, funny. Poets have been awkward: they have seemed funny. Coleridge, Shelley, Swinburne, among others, have seemed funny. The albatross manifests the unsuccessful bridging of two worlds poets' lives frequently contain. Walking and flying can stand for two kinds of consciousness which may collide and call each other names. The albatross contains enough of the farcical, tragical implications of unplanned doubleness.

79. *The Reason for Sweetie, A Cat's, Leaving Us in May 1959.* 1960. The going elsewhere of Sweetie, an amiable being I knew, simply must have its good significance. How can a pussycat change her mode of being without some change for the better in the way things are and do? And it would be unjust to Sweetie to say that in her, the intent to do good, changing things was not present. Sweetie was all good intent: a living being, a being, is good intent when seen as well as can be. Sweetie, then, looked for what she could do and show. One thing that this pussycat was for, was a greater kindness and honesty in various phases of United States administration. The American people became more interested in the ethical quality of various Washington personnel through what was ascertained about the falling of a plane near Sverdlovsk, Russia, on May 1, 1960, almost exactly a year after Sweetie's taking herself elsewhere. Evidence then of a strong kind points to our pussycat's having much to do with the ethical lesson mentioned. Chronology is there, but there is more: the character of this pussycat, her development, significance, conduct: profound beginning. The poem then is historically scrupulous.

79. *Prayer of a Secretary of Defense in Pain.* 1966. In recent years some people have felt evil could be in an American Secretary of Defense. The name of this Secretary of Defense is McNamara. McNamara was one of a number of people who, being financially adept and well placed, thought it was right to put down by force another mode of making a living, of using the economic world than the one they had used so achievingly. To do this, McNamara and people like him had to be cruel and utter insincere gabble about high causes—when what they were interested in was the safeguarding of their possessive selves. McNamara was instrumental in causing pain, disability for hundreds, hundreds of people in Vietnam. And then the Secretary of Defense was in pain himself with a twisted ankle. It is useful

157

to think of McNamara having pain somewhat like the pain he so readily caused and consented to in others. God, Christ, and poetic justice say it is proper to think of an American Secretary of Defense having pain as a means of understanding it better in others.

80. *I Should Love to Be Loved, By Endre Ady.* 1968. Man wants to be alone and also loved; he wants to be alone and also love. It is easy in Hungary or anywhere to feel that one is not cared for, not in the life of another or others at all. The Hungarian poet, Endre Ady, once thought this in Central Europe, and instead of just having a thought, stated the thought rhythmically; in apparently choice, melodious Hungarian. (Some melody goes from one language to another.) How does this poem exemplify Aesthetic Realism? It is because Aesthetic Realism says that essentially different attitudes of self are in an aesthetic relation: that the desire for complete individuality is the same as the desire to love fully and accurately what is not oneself; for through another life, individuality is wholly what it is. Therefore, when Ady is stating the two possibilities and wishes of self, he is doing what is necessary if one is to see later that one can be just what one is and "of someone" on the same Tuesday. Aesthetic Realism says that the outside world exists to sharpen, complete, affirm individuality not to dilute it. Self and World, Aesthetic Realism believes, are two opposites like Color and Outline, Oneness and Manyness, Nearness and Remoteness which have been one in art; can be one in ourselves tomorrow.

81. *The First Amendment and the Red, White and Blue.* 1956. The First Amendment to the Constitution of the United States of America is a beautiful attempt of a country to establish freedom for the people living in it. We don't know what freedom is, but the First Amendment has freedom for its legal music; has freedom as lasting substance. Man is Being, Response, Expression, and if he doesn't have the third of these truly, the other two have to suffer, have to become less. The First Amendment says that men may be wrong, that men who govern, legislate, preside over courts may be wrong, and if so, other men may say so in a way that makes the perhaps wrong representatives of a nation become attentive, thoughtful, and, it may be, even, different. It is fitting that the Amendment which has in it the right to criticize those who govern be given a lilt, a dash, a musical quality like that to be found in a judicious children's game. And if you don't love the First Amendment with impetuosity and permanence, you and love could be on better terms.

81. *Quaint Type and Whirlingness.* 1943. It is hard to say how related things are, how they are of each other, how they are the same. Impetuous and inclusive perception can see space and time in little crumbs whirling through words of well-fashioned lips. The present world is the world as seen by us: how else can it be seen and still be the present world? Cannot

Colonels hear words with space and time in them, and cannot the Colonels note them? We should know what this means before we say it cannot be. How can past and present be to each other? Where else can the eighteenth century be? Do we really have new clouds, since the clouds of now are so much like eighteenth-century clouds? And how akin are rhetoric and crumbs and whirlingness in the beginning of the world, which of course we still have, for that which is now is only the contemporary form of the beginning of the world. We might as well say that a body doesn't exist because each day it is attired otherwise, garbed differently. Pshaw! If existence is seen as, powerfully, sameness, there are the drums of softness and the giant sound of sweet lips. In sameness, nouns and adjectives can be anything. And with existence as sameness, quaint type will tell of us years later, as quaint type will tell of whirlingness and time. Philosophy says, You can do anything with sameness; and existence without sameness as a base is impossible.

82. *Rather Sighed For.* 1927. While existence is sameness, unutterable oneness, it also is excitement, melodrama, surprise. We are for the utmost stir and the utmost nonchalance. Think of reality with millions of cubic miles of nothing but space, and of reality with volcanoes and much volcanic ash. What speed can be in reality! What collisions! What things can show speed! How friendliness can be accompanied by speed and speed! What possibility of multiple racingness! Within us is a desire for tumult, revolution, even catastrophe. The other desire is there too: the desire to be unquestionably composed. Existence has varied with its explosiveness and with its monotony. It is now necessary to study existence as frightful and not off the ground. It is hoped this poem will assist.

82. *By the Wave.* 1958. Existence is that in which the lost and had are always in a quiet battle: where the gone and present are in an unheard contest—sometimes heard. The last motion of a wave is immediately something else—and so water and waves are the sad contrary to inscriptions in bronze or on mountainsides, or of strong print or of lasting script. We don't know what is lost. Let me mention some things. We may have lost an epigram of Helen. We may have lost some notes of Beethoven, heard by him in sleep and then not heard. A tremendously beautiful mumble of Cromwell may have been lost. Shakespeare's best soliloquy is, fairly certainly, with the absent. The best moments of most lives have, it may justly be said, not found words now available. So the wave in the poem may be saying what is necessary. Repetition saves the rising and falling of water: there is not such repetition to save other things, communicable things.

82. *A Moose Moves.* 1957. Does thought move the way the visible, living and bulky moves? In this poem, an inference is seen as moving the way a moose does in a forest. An inference is a deduction from and a going

159

from facts seen as existing or acceptable. Three raincoats seen on three people in the same street and in the same half hour could make for the inference that three people had thought it would rain. Once the inference is seen as having been made, it is also seen as having moved from something—as a moose might from the darkness or shadow of a number of trees. And some inferences are startling: they emerge from the facts—maybe the once dim facts—in a surprising way. The import or value of an inference moves through or in one's mind as a moose might. The moose is so definite once it is seen; the motion of a moose is so different from the rest of the woods. Facts make for inferences, which may make for hypotheses, which may make for theories, which may make for verifications; all which may make for science. The Darwinian theory at one time began with an inference: it had to. All this about inferences and theories is not against the steady walk of a moose out of woods; and now, before our eyes, through woods. (Appeared in *Today's Japan*, 1959.)

83. *For the World.* 1926. To live is to protest against the world and its cause. We protest against the world because the way it affects us does not please us: there may be too much of the world oppressing us; but also we feel sad and reproachful because something essential in the world, its possible friendliness, is not ours. If we give Wordsworth's "The world is too much with us" a meaning different from Wordsworth's own but which the sentence can bear; and if we take the four Hebrew words included in the Greek of the New Testament (Matthew 27), "Eli, Eli, lama sabachthani?"—God, God, why have you forsaken me?—we have the two general human dissatisfactions with the way of the universe or God. We look for change, but the change we look for we do not see—"painful snow came when we thought joy would." We wish for an entirety of feeling—"whiteness" of feeling—but that is not ours. However, the complaint in the poem is supposed to have a praising largeness and affirming majesty of outlook. It is hard to see where the world is amiable to us, yet "we are yours, O world, come to us as you wish." In the last three lines of the poem, the desire to like the world illimitably and the desire to complain of it freely, clearly, bravely—both of these are there. It is the intention of the poem, through its music, to see the world as magnificently and subtly equivalent to oneself, even as that self is impelled to ask why this should be so, and to say this should not be so. It is a poem with, it is hoped, a junction through music of unhindered affirmation and not-stopped-at-all negation.

83. *Tree, By Asia, By the Sea.* 1927. Winds and ocean in relation to trees on shore have for a long time made for a sadness in the human mind that can be described as Wailing Geography. Some of this wail or piercing sadness is in Mendelssohn's *Hebrides*. The loneliness of man is to be seen in a tree of northern Europe having winds go through it, with these winds also over ocean, ocean that is near. For the branches of a single tree to be shaken by a wind which later is the Atlantic's, is something about man sur-

rounded and reached by forces which come from afar, come from the depths, and go to the boundaries of earth and the world. A tree is affected by all space or air in motion; and we are affected by mentally blowing reality. To think of what man is affected by is to meet sadness and largeness. How large, inclusive, is what affects me?—can be valuably asked by anyone. When the poem says, "For all winds are with each other," it is like saying all things affecting us have something in common, have a relation among themselves. Beginning with a tree in Scotland, with the Atlantic near, is like beginning with a person by himself but with everywhere acting upon him. The near of Scotland becomes the sea and Asia; and ourselves in our intimacy are reached by causes and motions from sources standing for north, south, east, west in reality. There is crying here; there can be exultation.

84. *Something Else Should Die: A Poem with Rhymes.* 1968. The purpose of art and of politics, in the long run, can be described as the same: the defeat of ugliness. Ugliness is the failure of a good general meaning or possibility of the world to be the same as the attitude, the motion, the intent, the doing of an individual or individuals. John Wilkes Booth seemed to override the intent of America with his intent: the killing of Lincoln made for a while an ugly individual attitude supreme. It was so with the killing of Martin Luther King. Is it not felt by the contemporaries of John Wilkes Booth and by the contemporaries of the unascertained killer of Martin Luther King that these killers are ugly? Ugliness is interference with beauty as large by the narrow which, for the while, is stronger. Injustice will die only when an individual no longer can feel that individuality is more served by injustice than by justice; by ugliness rather than non-ugliness. Certainly the lessening of injustice looks good—as a tree does or a paragraph may.

84. *Because.* 1958. We have two directions: one for the self trying to please itself narrowly, exclusively, owningly; the other which tries to please a self aware of the whole world as a cause and the whole world as useful company. In the effort to be pleased intimately with ourselves, we may fall by the wayside, even though it seems we are achieving something. Pain is deceptive, and a thorny bush may look like something else. Often, for one thing, to be hurt is an accomplishment for the person who glories in the enmity of what is not himself to what is. If there is no desire to be dissatisfied with what is external, the thorny bush is less likely to attract. We think we want to be pleased by one thing after another; we think we want everything to make us happy—but if, in being happy, we are diminished in importance to ourselves, in importance as we see importance, we can take unhappiness as against happiness. Aesthetic Realism sees importance and happiness as two things in every person not going for the same purpose or conclusion. This adds so much to the heterogeneity or discord of emotion.

84. *Jolly Poster Poem.* 1955. The *Jolly Poster Poem* is a rousing mani-
festo for past American superficiality, also for superficiality of the present.
—The *New Yorker* has been superficial, jokes and all.—If Lippmann has
not been so superficial, the cause he has been allied with has been and is:
this cause is the private exploitation of the world.—The *New York Times*
has often served injustice and unseemliness.—The Free World has been
one of the deepest, widest, most permeating frauds in history, and there-
fore, at the least, deserved a saraband with its name. The trouble with
the Free World is profound misuse of the adjective by people thinking
themselves in the Free World.—The word *totalitarian* has also been un-
relentingly misemployed by editors and other likely sloppy persons.—
"Oyster supper" and "vigilance" in the last item, instance the double
presence of a seeming sociality and of a cruel protectiveness in many per-
sons. The *Jolly Poster Poem* is a false invitation to find truth.

85. *Summer Again in New Jersey.* 1957. The particular States this land
has, show themselves differently and all interestingly, in summer. New
Jersey, being near New York City has a motor and green hullabaloo in
summer, within which hullabaloo are New Jersey traffic officers. Right
under a cloud in the New Jersey summer is one of these officers. As this
officer looks—it is his job to look—there are trees with leaves near, not
regardful of traffic obligations at all. These leaves are close to speed—the
many kinds of speed there may be in a New Jersey summer. So, there is
gasoline in the New Jersey summer—something maybe the seasons did not
look for once. Gasoline and leaves are somewhat incongruous, but they
are together in all the States, of a summer. Connecticut in summer is near
to New Jersey in summer. As we think of Minnesota and Michigan, we get
a feeling different from the New Jersey and Connecticut feeling—though
these three, "gasoline, cops, clouds," we may be sure, are there. The blue
in the sky of New Jersey and of Minnesota seem different. At this moment
we can ask: What are New Jersey and Minnesota? Along with all this,
there are people alone and in crowds. Being alone is motory; and a crowd
is motory. If this doesn't have a meaning, reality is wasting its time; and
it is ever so hard to be convinced of any instance of reality's wasting its
time.

86. *Every Evening.* 1927. Every evening of the world has been different,
but every evening has had something a little disorderly again and again.
Eleven men walking are not a symmetrical sight, but every evening has had
eleven men walking in it ever since evenings were. Moreover, not only
have a countless sequence of evenings had eleven men walking in them,
but have had the eleven men walking on a leaf-strewn road—and leaf-
strewn is another instance of the quietly disorderly. Weather, with which
evenings are in league, is sufficiently diverse in the world to have some
region always endowed with the falling of leaves there. Number, weather,

disorder, therefore, are inseparable from evenings on this earth. Since the purpose of poetry is to keep up with earth, this poem has a right to be in the present neighborhood.

86. *The Lesson of Art.* 1954. *The Lesson of Art* continues what is within the poem about Eleven Men Walking Every Evening on a Leaf-Strewn Road. That poem's intent was to make the unsymmetrical symmetrical through constancy or recurrence. In the present poem, it is said that symmetry cannot be absent from anything. Recent art has shown a pattern in the casual, the crowded, the jumbled, the messy, the weltering. The pattern is there—for the messy has number, and there is no number without some pattern; and the messy has difference, and there is no difference without some sameness. Debris, then, studied, will have number in it and sameness and difference. Symmetry is sameness and difference, with sameness seen as predominating. To say strongly or boldly or continually that the objects in a mess have the mess in common, is to give an early symmetry to the mess. To say that the objects in a mess are all of them less than an inch in size—which may very well be—is to see symmetry in the mess. To see and say that none of the objects or ingredients of debris is purple—and this may well be—is to give some symmetry to the debris. To think of the ingredients of debris as touching each other, or close, or being on the same floor, or sweepable or movable at once, is to give sameness or symmetry to the untidy collection. The poem, then, begins carefully.

86. *Hymn, By Charles Baudelaire.* 1967. Critics have not sufficiently asked how Baudelaire, while doubtful of women in other poems, a savage questioner of them, should have written a poem, *Hymne,* as praising of women as Spenser ever was, or Shelley in *Epipsychidion,* or Petrarch in some sonnets, or Dante in the *Paradiso.* The utmost that can be said for a woman or for women is in the five quatrains of Baudelaire beginning with *A la très chère, à la très belle.* In the third line of the poem, Baudelaire calls a woman an angel with all the lighted sobriety one might wish; and when Baudelaire says in the fourth line of the first quatrain, *Salut en l'immortalité!*—Hail in immortality!—he is somewhat beyond both Longfellow and Rupert Brooke in seeing woman with deep favor. And Baudelaire has his taste for eternity made keener by a woman. She makes existence deeper, sharper, more inclusive in the third quatrain. And in the fourth, a woman is an invisible something at the beginning of Baudelaire's immortality—*Au fond de mon éternité!* A woman in the last stanza is both Baudelaire's joy and health—*Qui fait ma joie et ma santé.* What has Baudelaire's *Femmes Damnées* to do with this unrestrained praise of woman in the neat resonance of the French quatrain, profound and symmetrical? —For the while, it should be said that the Baudelaire revering the meaning of woman is as true a Baudelaire as the Baudelaire of corrupt corpses, imperiously fleshly females, iniquity in the last stories of large Parisian dwelling houses, cats with a leaning to evil, and the heart of the poet

163

leering as Satan leers. Sunrise, too, is in Charles Pierre Baudelaire, and
the sunrise is a lady—in this *Hymn.*

87. *Murder Is Told Of.* 1932. This poem, while maintaining the pro-
cedure, somewhat, of the detective story, is about how we murder something
in ourselves, assisted, it may be, by others. The worst function of a friend
or of someone we know is to consent to or encourage the putting aside or
diminishing or annulling of a possibility of ourselves. The whole world
knows that Macbeth said he had murdered sleep—so what else can be
murdered? The lawyer Greening is that in us which wants to be correct
and whose mode of being correct may, even with some justification, be
opposed by us. In the poem, then, something in us has been killed with
the encouragement of another. A quiet, unseen happening is given the
narrative panoply of a mystery. The tale in free verse is negative, for the
murderer is, after ten years, not found. There are many stories about
ourselves, the center of which is Not, or It Was Possible and Wasn't. The
poem aims to have a certain clipped and lingering narrative music, while
being descriptive of mind unregarded.

88. *Seem to Do Most.* 1964. Sensation takes place in many ways. It is
clear that if a cold wind comes to our face of a November night, we don't
have much to do with it: we are just the recipient of the cold wind and
have the appropriate sensation. However, when our thumb presses paper
there is a sensation, and we seem to do most of the sensation work. Further,
as we do the sensation work, the thumb seems to be predominating; and
then there is the "you" of the poem, or ourselves, which can be seen as
apart from the thumb, while, to be sure, this "you" has the thumb. Sensa-
tion always separates something of oneself from oneself as complete and
instant. To taste something sweet is to have the mouth territory apart from
the rest of oneself. Even if one has a general sensation of tiredness or cold
or hunger, these may be seen as apart from the "you" or oneself having
them. The apartness is felt in a particular way when we are active in the
getting of sensation—as we are when our thumb presses on paper. How
our existence is asserted when a thumb of ours presses on paper should be
considered: it is important, and speaks well of life and existence. The poem
is a bit of propaganda for the best part of our unconscious: the feeling or
possibility of feeling that our life is a particular, loving conquest of reality.
(Appeared in *Definition*, 1964.)

88. *1960 Regret Poems.* 1960. The history of politics is compelled to
study nullity or, at least, the diminution of meaning. At this moment,
American politics is fraught with nullity and meaning; the preponderance,
I believe, being for meaning. The American election of 1960 was essen-
tially a confrontation of nullity or the absence of value. One contender was
evil minded with, being less strong than all the American forces, a large

likelihood of welcome ineptness. The other was more generous minded, but with a strong tendency to put aside the generous mindedness and go with the unethical political and industrial current. Evil and good came to equal strength in the two unappetizing contenders, and the way evil and good could submerge each other in the contenders made the election a great stall, or a transitory nullity. We have gone beyond this. Meaning is walking the street and knocking on hitherto quiet doors. Time can be more valuable than candidates—time with its full meaning. Time does knock off Poskudnaks, or unhandsomely selfish people. We are beyond the impasse of November 8, 1960, when two persons, neither of whom deserved it, went for the nation's acclamation. There was not an election, because there was nothing substantial to choose. To use one of the most ordinary phrases in the States, it was six of the one and a half-dozen of the other. The nullifying impasse is now over, it can be hoped, and American politics does not consist so much of one kind of evil pitted against another kind of evil, but somewhat evil as against a discernible love of good. The present deep turbulence in America arises from the feeling that a hero, albeit dim, uncertain, somewhat shuffling, is against a National Dragon, Selfishness, organized all these years in township and state.

89. *Kangaroo.* 1927. There are two questions about the kangaroo, arising from whatever may be the cause of the world and the manner of its doing things. If God is the cause of the world, it is necessary to believe he either foresaw the existence of the kangaroo or could have foreseen it. And God also would have thought it better that the kangaroo be in Australia, and not in Idaho or Maine; and also God would foresee the manner the kangaroo would have of moving, remaining still, affecting things. God simply has to see all things or be able to see all things, should he choose. It is quite clear, then, that it is not too much to have God say that he knew the kangaroo would be. We know that the kangaroo is. God knows that the kangaroo is, but he also knew, once, that it would be. If God is not the cause of the world, then the kangaroo would be implicit in either the cause of the world or the world itself. The world somehow arrived at the kangaroo and the kangaroo's location. What enabled the world to have a kangaroo and the kangaroo's location must have existed long before the first jump of the kangaroo. Knowledge, then, of the kangaroo is nearest to implicit being, which, as being and as implicit, had the kangaroo within it. God makes it simpler: he knew about the kangaroo's being all the while there was a while, or there was time, or there was eternity. The kangaroo and eternity are inseparable.

89. *Horror Can Use Horror When Ethics Fails.* 1968. Maybe the Hanoi government wanted to tell how the people of Hanoi felt as they were bombed. So the rocketing of Saigon began. In this world horror and ethics are as different as anything; and with astonishing reality behavior, can be alike, close, the same. We should know about this more.

90. *Which Fires.* 1928. The rain and fire of the world are concerned with humility and arrogance in man; with his meltingness and haughty dryness. It is hard to think of divinity as humble, yet when divinity found it right to have the undivine in reality, divinity was humble; indeed, divinity is humble now. How did God in his majesty come to rain? Why does tremendous reality have to have rain? Soft rain is an aspect of a scientific and godly universe; the universe, then, is yielding and divinity is multitudinously gentle. Justification for that statement man will simply not disavow—God is love—is to be found in the arrogant manifestations of reality and their gentleness. Love is sweetness felt as strength; and when divinity drizzles, love can be seen there, even with a little ridiculousness. Fire and mist have been regarded as attributes of the Lord as geography, physics, and meteorology. Fire and mist, or blaze and soft rain are, as one thing, an attribute of functioning deity. And our fire and our meltingness, our conflagration and our gentle rain are of one central thing in ourselves. The poem is concerned with these considerations.

90. *The Laurels Are Cut Down, By Théodore de Banville.* 1967. One of the great lines of French poetry is Théodore de Banville's *Nous n'irons plus au bois, les lauriers sont coupés.* Within the sound of this line, of these words, is the message of many autumns to a self not sure of where it is in the world. The becoming of the world colder is something which can bring a person close to musical nothingness. The gorgeousness of things may change to outline. Water with sun in it may change to severe, non-caressing crystals. The stag may be fearful, hinting oneself should be. The grass is withdrawn, and would no more luxuriate than deliver a forceful oration. The laurels are cut down, and we have a feeling we know what we exactly are, when the reckoning is in; and we don't like it. What better can we do with what we don't like than make poetry of it? This Banville does; the consequence is fine for poetry in general. And when poetry in general is at its finest, it always refutes somehow, somewhat, the idea of the world as a desolating enemy to man.—Housman used the first line of the poem, and Banville may have been instigated by some words he met. All we are doing is to state what the poem has in it, as we now have it.

90. *Free Earth.* 1927. Reality is the freest thing there is: it is its own law, its own whim, its own motion; at least, as God it is these. If God is to be seen as author of reality, then God is the freest thought of ours, for he is the freest cause. In both reality and God, however, we can feel, see, perceive law at its utmost, its most subtle and mighty. The name Manoona in the poem is an amphibrach as prosody, with freedom at its beginning, *ma;* substance as the accented, lingering syllable, *noo;* and freedom once more in the lively, lightsome *na.* The name, though, is not Sanskrit, but English. Early in the poem, shakings of nerves are related to a world that can do anything and be anything. And then, there are four possibilities of existence brought together, some intimate and some with distance. Fallings,

smiles, grins, hardenings are all instances of reality as doing. Other things mentioned are quick studies in possibility and likelihood: the mind can welcome the customary and credible in the same minute that it sedulously dallies with the unlikely, even the unheard of. The world allows the boring, the faintly interesting, and the sheerly imagined. It is an allowing world, a free earth, Manoona is told, and it is hoped Manoona herself is the likeness of an allowing world and a free earth. The odds are, she is such a likeness.

91. *Roland and the Archibishop: From the* Chanson de Roland. 1964. Perhaps early in the second half of the twelfth century in France a poem was written which has great narrative dignity and a succinct musical dignity also great. The lines end in words resembling each other in sound while they have a visual and auditory existence by themselves. The *Chanson de Roland* has lines which thump delicately as they merge with each other. Every step of the poem, that is, every line was looked on by the writer as something to be breathless about. Other poems accent flow—poems of Yeats and Mallarmé do—but the *Chanson de Roland* accents the line with its own life and prosodic beat: there is flow, but the beat is what we see first. The part of the *Chanson de Roland* translated has a scarcity of subordinate clauses: these make for glide or continuity of sound. Each line, nearly, contains a separate action. The separate action is usually followed by another separate action. Music can come this way, for music can be like separate boulders in a field. As we look at the line

> Last, he held him embraced to his breast
> (*Contre sun piz puis si l' ad enbracet*)

the mediaeval French is definite, hard; but so kind in definiteness and hardness, so tearful. And as Roland goes looking for the dead bodies of people he knew, juttingness and compassion are indissoluble. The dying Archbishop Turpin whom Roland has just left so that he can find friendly bodies, speaks in a way that has the softness of thoughts about death along with the grievousness of these thoughts. "Saintly flowers" in paradise are so close to ill fortune. The *Chanson de Roland* is grand in how it meets one of the possibilities and demands of poetry: the showing of this world as forbidding and gentle, harsh and kind, ever so sharp, ever so comprehensively annulling.

92. *Duval Is on the Run: The People Are on the March, By José María Quiroga Pla.* 1937. Some poems were written by persons in Spain, as, in 1936, Francisco Franco and his fascist associates and assistants were doing all they could to destroy the rather democratic government of Spain.—It is well known that a good cause may not make for so good a poem; but the lines of José María Quiroga Pla about a discomfited fascist general, have satire,

167

largeness of feeling, earthiness, space, motion in a manner distinctive of poetry. The music of kind and powerful victory is in the poem. When the people wait for General Duval—"The people waited for him at Naval-peral"—a place name mingles with an emotion in a manner that is grand and tingling. We feel that when the poem says: "The red flower of Spanish blood"—it is that. And the retreating general, in the sanctity of personal and governmental reaction, is put in motion with auditory and visible impact. The democratic feeling of Spain—apparently there now—is presented strongly, but without "proletarian" truculence and lack of aesthetic substance. When we are told of "the stones of the Sierras and the rivers, heavy in their flowing," while we are in the midst of the ordinary man's courageous anger, we are with the verbal might, too, of *Chevy Chase*, Burns, and the Byron of certain stanzas of *Childe Harold*. We are also with melodious and forceful lines of the Spanish *cancionero* of centuries ago. Yes, poetry is here, and it is functioning against Francisco Franco, and can still. The poetry of Spain is always waiting to be used again. (Appeared in *And Spain Sings: Fifty Loyalist Ballads Adapted by American Poets*. Edited by M. J. Benardete and Rolfe Humphries. New York: The Vanguard Press, 1937.)

93. *The Umpires Are There, With Their Fair and Foul.* 1968. The American people is governed (like other peoples) by a desire for America to be right and also by a desire to be fair. When patriotism and fairness are one, a patriotic nation is happiest; and nearly every nation is patriotic. The desire Americans have had for their country to be right and victorious is most appealing. Occasionally, however, the not so searching person comes to have a feeling that what seems to be his country is not right. Such a large and inclusive thing as a country may of itself never be wrong; but when a country is propelled and managed by private, not national interests, the appearance of that country may be in error. Never were there before such misgivings as to fair and unfair, right and wrong as have been in American minds in the last years. In every state, there have been plenty of people whose sense of fairness was hardly satisfied with what their representatives were doing. The number of these people has been increasing. Many Americans have had the feeling that if there were an Umpire standing for the whole world, an Umpire with the discernment and comprehensiveness of the Divine Being, this Umpire would murmur, also shout, Foul! as he saw what American representatives were doing in Asia. The poem says that what makes an American see fairness or foulness in a game of basketball or baseball has been displeased by the doings in Southeast Asia. America, like a crowd in a stadium, has been uttering and yelling Foul! to persons who act as if they were doers of the American will, representatives of American intent.

94. *A Sentence of Sir Thomas Browne in Free Verse: A Found Poem.* 1967. Death and time are two friends permitted by existence, cherished by

existence, and externalized as mysterious by existence. Existence is a kind of showman. If death and time cannot cause a mighty, wide, keen emotion in one, it cannot easily be presumed that anything can. Death and time caused an emotion notable in English literature, within the apprehensive and meditative mind of Sir Thomas Browne, there in the seventeenth century. It has been thought, and rightly, that some searching and resonant prose is in the early sentences of the Fifth Chapter of Browne's *Urn Burial*. When we hear these sentences justly, we can discern the musical, organized, informative labyrinth prose can be. Particularly the first sentence of the chapter has been chosen as the material for learned ah's. There is no doubt that this sentence has not been neglected. Yet one possibility was not made the most of. How would the sentence be, how would the sentence sound in Free Verse? It seems that the most distinguished prose in English can be transmuted into Free Verse with both prose and verse honored. What happens when the first sentence of the Fifth Chapter of *Urn Burial* is put into Free Verse is this: the elements of the sentence are given a more definite life of their own, while still they are continuous; there is more of a dramatic juxtaposition between say, "Methuselah" and "yard under ground"; one can look at "outworn all the strong and specious buildings above it" with a neater response to narrative entities within the daring and elaborate sentence. Moreover, it is well to have prose and verse becoming each other when, by doing so, they say something about the nature of prose, the nature of verse—and both prose and verse are modes of beauty. Prose, it would please Sir Thomas Browne to consider, is the universe uninterrupted and flowing; verse is the universe apportioned, given comely detail, appropriate segments, beseeming, independent aspects.

95. *Fine Ethical Moment of Charlie Barnes.* 1958. A quiet and sad aspect of human history is the undervaluing by many, many persons of their best and most useful perceptions. It does seem as if, judging from how people have been, contempt was something more usable as a builder up of the ego or concealed self than respect or deep like. We all know that if we have a deep and true feeling, we should externalize it accurately and strongly; but as the world has been, and as something in us has been, it is easy to go away from a feeling we have had through our own perception, not because it is "in the air" and has evident, multiple, and powerful advocacy. Charlie Barnes in the present two stanzas is wiser than has been the custom. He proclaims a good feeling, though unusual, because he knows he himself has had it. Most often, we do not associate our unsustained perceptions, however sincere for us, with the possibility of affirming both ourselves and the truth of things. Charlie Barnes at this time is too much of an ideal. We have to hope that he becomes a usefully, sweetly crushing actuality. The Casey Jones rhythm of the lines, we are sure, will help.

95. *Still the Dawn.* 1957. *Still the Dawn* is a cultural narrative in six lines, each of which is an instance of that godly foot in prosody, the

amphimacer. The poem tells of how light or knowledge—here termed dawn—came to man and man was afraid of it. Man does show his endlessly profound doubleness in his going for knowledge always, and his being afraid of knowledge, also. So man runs from the dawn. But things can't terminate this way. Man has to like the light adequately, even sudden light, light he thinks he isn't prepared for. The dawn, light, or knowledge by their very nature have to wait.—Reality spends a good deal of its time waiting. Reality by its very nature has to wait. Man sees himself as waiting, but doesn't see something besides him wait. If nothing waited for man, wouldn't man have the right to feel insulted on the matter?

95. *Two Stanzas from French Literature about Death: In* Stances à Du Perrier, *By François de Malherbe*. 1950. It is one of the fine possibilities of poetry, to join the stately and the tender. In poetry the sedateness and nobleness of a temple may be deeply mingled with the tear of friendliness and the trembling of love that is near. The French poet Malherbe, chiefly known for his stateliness, his unrelenting verse architecture, has for many years been regarded as one who also depicted death truly and tenderly. The tears of things are within the stately, resonant quatrains of Malherbe, whose manners as a person had something of the effective arrogance of Samuel Johnson and the jeering awareness of pretense given to Thomas Carlyle. Yet the presence of Malherbe, wisely arranged, can be of pleasing use to all. This use is within the music, thoughtfulness and lachrymatory wit of the first stanza translated. It simply lives, the stanza does, in French poetry, even with the advent of Mallarmé and Michaux. And the second stanza given English words is different from the first, because it is expansive; has a touch of history; includes renowned architecture. Yet this stanza also throbs accurately and intimately through the presence of ageless strings, honestly touched. If we give a most effective guitar to the formidable François de Malherbe—questioned by some as a poet—we shall not be unseemly at all.

96. *It and Beauty*. 1930. The ubiquity and multifariousness of beauty are looked at in this poem. The beauty we are after in all its unknownness and might, is allied to the comeliness of an insect leaping. All beauty says something of all other beauty. The beauty of a dull pond comments on the beauty of a grasshopper in lofty motion. If any beauty is served by any aspect of men's wars, this rather repellent beauty has a kinship to magnificent, unsmirched comeliness. Old hospitals may be beauty's servants. And form making for an emotion about reality itself is too strong for books and a person to interfere with its ability to set nerves astir or certain fragments. Beauty is of physics, and physics is about what matter does and has done to it. Everything we have, the poem says, is in favor of beauty. Let us see if this is true at all, and, then, how much it is true.

96. *Monologue of a Five-Year-Old.* 1963. In the *Monologue of a Five-Year-Old,* some of the self-satisfaction of a child less than six is given an equivalent in line structure. The lines are meant to be trim, smug, and threatening. The child talking is convinced that the adults in her life don't deserve much; are worthy of being profoundly bothered. The grim juvenile doesn't think her parents are just to her, so why be sacrificial and yielding? Fun is the thing to make of parents. The parents we have in the poem maneuver with each other, so why cannot a dispassionate young person maneuver with them? Plots are discerned by the preschool strategist, so why not add a plot of one's own? Pretense is a common choice; consequently it is right to make fun of pretending people and to defeat them.— The five-year-old is replete with keenness and disgust, disgust and keenness. Should one not put one's discoveries, perceptive and affective, to use? The answer is a sly and pervasive, Yes. (Appeared in *Definition,* 1963.)

97. *The Fall of the Leaves, By Charles Hubert Millevoye.* 1967. There are many sad poems in the world, and only a few of these have affected people for a long time, and clearly, and deeply. When a poem is taken to themselves by many people, one can say that it is the obviousness and ordinariness of the emotion that have made for this effect. Immediately, the question is with us: if it is only obviousness and ordinariness of emotion that make a poem liked conspicuously and lengthily, why do not all the obvious and ordinary poems succeed with a superficial and undiscriminating public? There must then be something about an ordinary and obvious poem which achieves popularity with the populace that the obvious, ordinary poems not achieving this don't have. And we find that this differentiating thing in the popular field is form, structure, aesthetics, fashioning—the way these are essentially in more "distinguished" or "subtle" works. The mind of man, which means the mind of every man, is somewhat subject to aesthetic emotion.—And so, when *La Chute des Feuilles* of Charles Hubert Millevoye appeared in France in the early part of the nineteenth century, the public found something different and strong in this sad poem; and the public can find it again. The lines of Millevoye are dense with emotion, but dense with structure too. The slowness of the poem instigates tearfulness, but this slowness also is poetically accurate, powerful. A line like *Tombe, tombe, feuille éphémère!* is abrupt and lasting at once. This line has in it the possible likeness of a person to autumn going towards winter. This is ordinary, but is it true? Can the ordinary truth become aesthetically piercing? The Millevoye poem is an early instance of the general Romantic tendency to make nature and self one thing; to make the growing and fading external world like what we are. Millevoye here has a permanent music, though this music first was heard in Napoleonic days. The music is there, ready to reach selves and ears.

98. *Note on Circles and Spirals.* 1961. We can valuably impute attitudes to anything. If we honestly ask how something, whatever it may be, feels,

the question may be looked at as ridiculous, but it is not useless (the ridiculous is hardly the same as the valueless). Should we ask how the Pacific Ocean feels, we may quite appropriately think we are ridiculous, but we couldn't say that asking this question has no use for us. Trying to see how the Pacific Ocean might feel broadens the mind, exercises the imagination, expands awareness, and brings comprehensiveness to the heart. If the ridiculous can do all this, long live the ridiculous! Proceeding: in the same way as the feeling of the Pacific Ocean is surmised, one can ask how parallels look on a triangle. Since the present writer has already asked this, an answer is with us. Parallels look on a triangle antagonistically. Further inquiry is invited. The poem being dealt with is the result of a finding that, just as parallels are uneasy with triangles, circles are uneasy with spirals. An opposition exists between circles and spirals like that which exists between Greek mythology and Presbyterianism. There is a repose about circles which looks on the continuous industry in space of the spiral with immediate disfavor. The conclusion was come to from all this that circles don't like to be compared, even, with spirals. Such is the message of these four lines.

98. *Merriment Can Be an Object of Thought.* 1961. We can have a seventeenth-century person thinking of us if we use our imagination that way. Besides this, we can participate in all the merriment or high spirits of the past. Would anyone say that reading of an exuberant and witty Roman feast left him with nothing at all of exuberance, of Roman, of wit, of festiveness? What, after all, are we affected by when we read, if it isn't the thing we read about? And how much and how are we affected? If we give ourselves to ancient Roman jesting, it is that which comes to be of our life. Suppose there was a fine bit of Latin merriment and we read of it, or read it, carefully, deeply, inwardly—would not the merriment become as much a part of our lives as a color of now or a speech of now? However, if past merriment can affect us now, that past merriment is not over. It is hard to say, for it is hard to think, that what can affect us now doesn't exist at all; is over. The large question is whether we make something more alive by thinking about it. That it is there for us to think about shows that it is with reality; moreover, when a thing of once is thought about, ourselves and our thought are somehow added to that thing, unless we want to say that thought is nothing at all. An ontological, also epistemological problem of note is, How can it be said that something is completely ineffective, and how can it be said that what is not completely ineffective is not present? The poem now looked at intimates that the relation of cause, effect, existence, individual life can be scrutinized and comprehended in a larger way than what has been. Past merriment exists; can past merriment exist with the persons taking part being entirely null, entirely absent? What do we mean when we say something is absent? If, as has been said, reality is not absolute, or presence is not absolute, is then absence or unreality absolute? Again, the poem intimates that if we do

not apprehend absolute reality, we do not apprehend absolute absence either. This speaks well for past merriment, as of any time, including our own.

99. *The Poem of Catullus about Attis.* 1966. The Attis poem of Catullus, while being one of the important documents on warring forces within man, says something of poetry itself. Catullus, like some other Romans, could be delicate, tender, poignant in elegiacs; but there is a satirical directness in him, a personal way of attack, an unrestrained dismissal of the objectionable which have been associated with masculine restlessness and pugnacity. Catullus, when he fails, can be slashing without being poetic. When he is felicitously Catullan, as largely in this poem, the might of Rome quivers along with a dewy leaf in Northern Italy of a brisk, late summer morning. Catullus is sturdy as he trembles with subtle knowledge. Masculine and feminine are one in poetry in a more successful manner than they are in persons above sixteen. Poetry musically follows reality in its manifestations as aqueduct and ripple. When the masculine-feminine question, now so pervasive, insistent, is seen as beginning in fine and ponderous existence, in delicate and weighty substance, in trembling object—the study of man and woman will truly begin. When poetry, including the lyrics of Catullus, Tibullus, Propertius, Horace, is regarded as a valuable, indivisible junction of masculine and feminine, poetry instead of being seen as something arising from sex—as may happen—will be seen, as sex is, to be the attempt of man to make sense, harmonious, delightful, important sense, of the opposing things reality always has as constituents. Greek and Roman mythology sees sex as instancing the reality of water, mountain, plain, cloud, wind, light. The present poem of Catullus can be used to find poetry the oneness of masculine impetus and feminine quiet possibility. Catullus can be used to see sex as aesthetic composition and definition. Some other ways of seeing sex haven't done so well.

103. *Ballade Concerning Our Mistake and Knowledge of It.* 1960. Man is the only living being who can accuse himself of having made a mistake. Is this useful? The Ballade says it is, for there are worse things than thinking we made a mistake. A good deal of life is complaint, and would it not be wise to know just what we are complaining of? The outside world and other people may be mistaken and misery-giving; still, can we, through a mistake or mistakes, give ourselves misery? The history of persons largely consists of purposes put into action, and this followed by the seeing of the purpose or activity as not standing for us. A wish of ours may not be that which includes what we wholly are. A wish can serve the inclination of a part of ourselves, with the other part objecting painedly when the chance arrives and is clear. Unless we are ready to see that an intention of ours may be sorrowfully disagreed with later, we can go on and on adopting objectives not sufficiently ours. It is taken for granted that if we do something, we have heard from all in ourselves we need to hear from; but

173

this is not so. Consequently, the readiness to see and to assert our having gone for something not liked by all of ourselves is a necessity for lightness of heart and happiness. If we don't see clearly that we, too, can like a wrong road better than a right one, we shall have a tendency to make the betraying of ourselves continuously more solid and invincible. The being sure that we can be mistaken about ourselves and about the value of what we prefer to do is the first thing in our being just to our lives. All this is said in argumentative prose. The Ballade says something consonant in the Ballade form as the fifteenth century in France made it known to the world of then and later. Our Ballade has even a Prince talked to in it. Ethics and continuous rhyme may be as friendly as anything.

104. *Towards Homer: Free Verse, Beginning with the First Lines of Pope's Translation of the* Odyssey. 1966. The beginning of Pope's translation of the *Odyssey* has a trim power and does have more of Homer's controlled musical, geographical, and mythological wandering than is usually granted. Still, there is no doubt that a freedom, a casualness, a daringness in space and surmise Homer has, is not in the couplets of the Augustan major poet. It is also quite just to think of Chapman as too swarming and uncertain, and of the blank verse of Cowper and Bryant as somewhat too dignified in blank verse watchfulness. Putting Homer into English hexameters hasn't pleased sufficiently so far; and those pleased by Homer translated into archaic and mobile prose, would still say something more was possible. So what can Free Verse do? What are the possibilities of Free Verse as such and in translation? Free Verse corresponds to the casual and the controlled; and the casual and controlled were in the mind of the person best called Homer. Greek is quite good with the casual and controlled. You can begin with Pope's translation and reach for the Greek. Free Verse plays seriously. Here Free Verse plays with lines of Pope in order to approach the effect of the Greek.

104. *The Voyage, VIII; By Charles Baudelaire.* 1967. Baudelaire had moods, aspects, hours, times of day, possibilities. One mood of Baudelaire made him find existence utterly pure beneath the disturbing, the vile, the helter-skelter and the heavy. Baudelaire's poem *Hymn* sees a woman as beauty and right and loveliness and reality, all uninterfered with. In the present poem, the Unknown and New are given this utter likability: it is as if, with the unattractive something, there was, there to be ascertained by one if one is able, the unseen, unknown, new, and purely pleasing. Baudelaire was devoted to a kind of sharp absolute: which, being sharp, hid its absoluteness. When Baudelaire says "This land tires us," he implies there is a land which will not. This land being New is lively in its utterness. The voyage of the poem is not just towards nothingness, as with Leconte de Lisle, three years older than Baudelaire. Abstract existence is tingling and engaging before the multiple author of *Fleurs du Mal.* The first line of *Voyage, VIII* is a tremendous instance of rhythmical rousingness and

174

scope. Death, the old captain, lifts the anchor as if the Wonderful Reality Party, looked for by him and his friends, at last was definitely and unquestionably gone towards. No more biding; things are in motion with a sense of what they're in motion for. Baudelaire's death and voyage poem announces the death of torpor, dullness, incompleteness.

105. *La Salle, As Having You in Mind.* 1961. One of the most beautiful questions in religion is whether God thought of us before and as he created us. The Calvinist notion of predestination has in it in some fashion God's awareness of who we are and how we are. Should God not know us, it is still possible to have every person thinking of us; indeed, every thing. Imagination is that big. The universe can be a pool in which our reflection is to be found. It is well to use our imagination to have others think of us, and think of us kindly and fittingly. The poem chooses Robert Cavelier, Sieur de La Salle to think of us because the French explorer was so alone in an untravelled United States, and had so much distinguished leisure. We can be rather sure that La Salle, had he known us at all or in any way, would have thought about us. Would it not have been good to do so with all that water, all those trees, all that hitherto unseen land—and that continuous sky? Becoming decisive: we can think of being in the mind of Robert Cavelier, Sieur de La Salle. Further, if you see yourself in the mind of Louis the Fourteenth's transatlantic servant, you will be better off. The poem is simply sensible.

105. *The Wolf and the Lamb, By Jean de La Fontaine.* 1949. Jean de La Fontaine's *The Wolf and the Lamb* is one of the cruellest instances of literature. The poem or fable is doubly cruel, for while it tells of an unjust occurrence, it also intimates that there is a way or trend in the human mind undeviatingly unkind. La Fontaine tells us that between having one's way and being just, having one's way is more powerful. It has been so, ever so many times. The most dangerous and ugly possibility inherent in the individual as individual is that the desire to have one's way seems strong, while justice seems flat and interrupting. The wolf wants the lamb and the want itself is justice. This is the way we are. If a want increases, just because it does, the want may seem the more just, well placed, accurate, right. The unconscious tendency or likelihood of making our want the same as universal justice is the ugliest adjunct of the heart of man. It is so easy to find an inclination interesting and necessary; and it is so hard to see and care for what is proportionate, equitable, ethical—it is no wonder persons are angry with others and can see themselves with confusion, dimness, scorn, uneasiness, loathing, displeasure. Our desire may seem so powerful, beckoning; and later so unhandsome. Were the life of La Fontaine's wolf pursued in a novel, with the wolf, of course, endowed with the self-objecting-to system man has, we should see the wolf undergoing the doubts of a Julien Sorel or a Raskolnikov. We have the tendencies of the wolf of the

fable, but also the uncertainty this particular wolf has not been able to manifest, or permitted to manifest.

106. *Autumn Song, By Paul Verlaine.* 1966. The winds of autumn have affected many people sadly: the October wail in space made for restless mournfulness in many hearts or personalities. What Verlaine does in this poem is to make the unboundaried grieving of autumn air in motion neat, trim, architectural, self-contained. It seems that the purpose of autumn sighs is to come to one mind, become that mind, stay with that mind, while there seems to be some kind of movement. In the first trim stanza, the winds become violins—which already causes intimacy. The heart receives the autumn sighs and is appropriately affected with a grieving conservatism. And the sighs of autumn make one remember when one was sad before. In the third stanza, a person decides to go along with the wind and be like a leaf, be like a leaf which has died. When the poem is looked at carefully, it appears pretty much like a sad tempest or something, in a strictly personal teapot. This is where the power of the poem is, however. Something in motion is made equivalent to a mind which is only itself and in grief. The simplicity of the language furthers strongly the becoming by autumn wind of the equivalent of a grieving heart. It is necessary that this simplicity not be gone away from, for if it is, there will be a discrepancy between the sigh of autumn and the feeling of one man. In the last stanza, while going about is affirmed, air and autumn and oneself are closely alike. Unless vague grief is seen as trimness, I think the intent of Verlaine has not succeeded. The poem has the finger of autumn mournfulness touching a human finger and becoming like it.

106. *Reminiscential Questions.* 1957. It is likely a good thing has been happening to reading America in late years. This good thing is the increased ability and disposition to see an author as a person, subject to the mishaps of individuality, and yet a person who says something notable about the universe in its universality. We can see crotchets and smallness, and not forget proportion, novelty, largeness of mind. The uncertainties of writers do seem now so much less important than pages we have. The couplets in this poem are concerned simultaneously with the frailties of writers and the possible strength and enduringness of some words of theirs. It was felt that rhymes were a way of making literary persons present in a week day and in a century or two centuries. So the author of a large and eloquent history of England in the sixteenth century is given a mood, not just six volumes or so. Miss Brontë, to whom we owe the somber, keen, and ominously captivating Jane Eyre, is given for a while jauntiness, no less. The author of the *French Revolution* is given a smile—for one reason because smile and Carlyle rhyme. (Carlyle is more noted for his continuous, abandoned, subterranean laugh than for his smile.) Macaulay is endowed with a blasé gesture—Macaulay unlike Beau Brummell, is not customarily seen as blasé: more as elaborately, oratorically impelled. Blake is so dif-

ferent from Macaulay, but the author of the Prophetic Books was, though, as the couplet implies, troubled by his body. And did one of the great observers of England and London as ethics, pettiness and evil, have occasionally a mood that was far away, with the sunset of some unknown Greek, on the right island, from which to see and meditate on sunsets and distance? Well, we can be pretty certain that moods were in James Anthony Froude, defender of early Protestantism, and William Makepeace Thackeray, satirist of English Protestants conducting themselves in secular London and the secular shires.

107. *A Strong City Is Our God, By Martin Luther.* 1967. God is given a tangible and organized strength in this poem. Offhand, we would not see God as a city or fortress. For one thing, God is spiritual; and for another, he is not just a city but all reality—and does not one diminish God by making him an armed municipality? However, it was necessary that God be might as might was understood in the sixteenth century of Germany and Europe. Once the idea of the city as strength is accepted, Christ as the Just Man—somehow identified with the city—seems more able to combat both the trickery and obvious warlike strength of the devil. The city changes into kindness and strategy, able to defeat the devil's malice and maneuvering. The way Luther metamorphoses city into fortress, city into Christ, city into justice, city into happiness, city into kingdom, is poetic and ingenious. And religion, of course, fares well.

108. *To the Reader, By Charles Baudelaire.* 1964. Tertullian, Swift, Jeremiah, Baudelaire are alike in this: they are severe and constant reprehenders of the human way. In their fashion, each has a notion of what goodness is; one has to have a notion of purity if one is to be assured of one's condemnation. And Baudelaire was certainly taken by the immaculate and universal. In the unendurable aggregation of the iniquitous present in Paris, he saw the accompaniment of light: Death, for one thing, was the great dazzling cleanser; and Baudelaire could see death at will. The purport of the notable *To the Reader* is that if man were completely honest about what should not be liked in him, he would get to reality, including his reality, uncluttered. The catalogue of the ugly must be complete, complete, complete, and complete always and desiredly. If this catalogue is complete, the ugly would at last be looked at unflinchingly, and this means with conquering antagonism. It is then goodness would be the same as courage, as logic, as factuality, as force, as subtlety, as form, as inclusiveness, and as annihilating, sweet power. The preface to *Fleurs du Mal,* which *To the Reader* is, shows the intent of Baudelaire to omit nothing in the evil omnibus. All the tricks, disguises, eludings had to be seen. And that most common of evils is given saliency in the last stanza: Ennui. Ennui arises from the triumph the individual has in making existence uninteresting. This defeat of existence by individual non-responsiveness or

individual incomplete participation is effectively related to all the other evils. Disrespect of what is not the self can lead to injustice to any aspect of that tremendous living and inanimate territory which is not oneself. Baudelaire in this poem states what the future study of man's unconscious will be busy with.

109. *Discouraged People*. 1961. People like other objects can be seen as different; but there is a tendency stronger than we know to make them alike. How strong this is can be seen if we contemplate the Rocky Mountains without a photograph or a painting to help us. We shall find an inclination in us to make the mountains all the same size. It needs an effort to retain clear distinction of size or height. And so with tomatoes. We are told some are four inches in width, some two-and-a-half inches, and some one inch. Our mind proceeds drearily, however, to make them the same size, whatever that may be. People in amphitheatres, stadiums, subways are so easily seen as the same size, wearing the same things, and having the same outlooks or dispositions. This is strongly so when we look at "discouraged" or tired people going home in the subway. It is difficult to see one person as different from another: indeed, it is difficult to see one person as such. The congestion predominates over individuality. This is on the dreary side, but a thorough aesthetic study of difference and sameness as one will result in tingling and emancipating wonders.

109. *Sameness and Difference in a Tragic Play*. 1956. Every play is about sameness and difference as manifested by hoping and fearing persons. Closeness and clash are of the midst of drama, and these are the constant show and possession of ordinary reality. Because Othello and Desdemona are similar while seeing things dissimilarly, Iago is able to achieve his desire to have them quarreling and to hurt each other. Hurt, like evil, arises from sameness and difference being close without having the same purpose deeply. Shakespeare knew four eyes and two persons never saw wholly the same way. The fact that we'd like to agree with others while desiring to affirm our own mode of sight, is in *Othello*, as it is in social history. There is such an inclination to believe that the person we like sees the way we do. Love so far has fed more on sameness or imputed sameness than it has on that equally loving and composing thing, difference. How would Othello take a disagreement with him by Desdemona, not just on the subject of Cassio but on a subject other, and of weight? We don't get the feeling that Othello saw it as possible that Desdemona disagree with him, or that he would like it if she did. It is these matters about what we are and who we are that are in motion in the present lines—with Othello, Desdemona, father, Iago so conspicuous.

110. *Basho Translations*. 1967. No Japanese metaphysician has as yet been acclaimed by the speculative West. Japanese have found it hard to

be like Hegel or John Stuart Mill or F. H. Bradley. They haven't as yet been given to abstract, difficult, angular philosophic subsections. With all this, metaphysics has a fine time in the haikus of Basho and often in Japanese poetry as such. The pond in the most famous of Japanese haikus, is old and immediate. The pond is old and as of the day as one's breakfast that morning. The frog, before he jumps, is just Being; as he jumps, he is change or motion; or as Hegel might say, the frog is now Becoming. The splash includes depth and rise, singleness and manyness. Metaphysical concepts are keenly in seventeen syllables—concepts, that is, without which being could not be thought of.—In the second haiku, change of position is juxtaposed to no change in the weight of something, no change in the shape of something. The something is food, designated by and accompanied by a lunch-tray. A visible change occurs with the lunch-tray but not with the food, which has in it the concepts of possibility and use; in this instance, human use. Within difference and sameness, something takes place and something does not occur, or does not take place. The gifts of metaphysics are handled, if not expounded, by Basho.

110. *The Voice, By Henri de Régnier.* 1967. Henri de Régnier is not usually seen as a poet of piercingness and power. He is usually seen as a poet of urns, old gardens, and Renaissance remnants in late nineteenth-century France. This is unjust, for Régnier has enough of Job in him to be other than a depicter of outward and inward elegance. The distaste for an earlier loved person is in the present poem with musical bitterness and stylistic cuttingness and persistence. The soul, as it will, has objected to what love brought; or, if one wishes, the personality has found something fearful and undesired in the caress of the woman chosen for amorous blessing and value. A late symbolist poet says his "heart today is miserable and sullen." Everything seems "somber" and "everything seems vain." Falsity has been seen in love itself, that is why. When Régnier says that his "sadness comes from something further than myself," he is saying that the nature of the world as a whole, as affecting himself, and within himself too, makes love seem to be a dull, regrettable misleader, not a fulfillment. Régnier is hardly alone in saying this, but the way he says it in these four quatrains is honest enough, composed enough, immediate enough, and everlasting enough.

111. *Searing Epistemology; or, The One Thing to Do.* 1958. In keeping with the idea of poetry and beauty, is the idea of God. Poetry and beauty are the passive sources of the instances of these; they are also the forces making for these. And so we come from God rather quietly, and then God is our active creator. God is both Source and Force. Sometimes we think we are managed or pushed around or tricked by something strong, stronger and more mysterious than ourselves. At this time, "Life is a plot to make you think you are alive." It is all arranged for you without your asking. You are in a show you never thought about and don't make sense of now.

179

You are deceived into thinking you see something: here reality is the agent of the Great Arranger. And you yourself are arranged so that—because the plot we are talking of is so deft, quiet, adroit—you see yourself as an individual with the capability of doing something in your own right and for yourself. It is all reality-and-appearance deception and plot. The best thing that can be said about the plots which are near us and in us, including the one that makes one think he is an individual, is implied in the last line of this poem: "Let us enjoy all these plots." Maybe, if we enjoy the plots, we shall find we are not so much against them; and maybe, even, later, in some way hard to understand, we ourselves had something to do with their contriving.

111. Art Poétique, *By Paul Verlaine*. 1950. That music and sculpture are both arts and have both pleased the mind of man is sign sufficient that the indefinite and definite—which music and sculpture are—can both please. At various times or places in the world, the definite beckons more; and then the indefinite may. The definite and indefinite may appear variously or be accompanied diversely or use material that changes. In France, after Romanticism as then understood and after definite, classical, meticulous, imposingly charming Parnassianism, the Indefinite once more seemed the very thing mind wanted, or at least some minds. Paul Verlaine's *Art Poétique* is one of the great honorings of the Indefinite as large in reality, central in art. We either, in mind, want to touch a wall or get away from a wall touching us. The need to be in the unboundaried and intangible is just ours. This need for the wavering and not glaringly tidy is in the first line of Verlaine's call for the airy as real. When Verlaine in 1874 wrote *De la musique avant tout chose*, he was saying something different for French poetry. French poetry, while, when it was poetry, was always musical, had not said music was the principal thing. Justness and depth of perception, visual grasp, verbal flexibility and exactitude, largeness of sentiment—things such as these had been first. When Verlaine said music was before everything, he was correct, correct even for the past; but French poetry after this poem of Verlaine, knew it was going for something else, was on a path designated Music rather than Verbal Propriety or Proportionate Judgment. It was not that music did not care for these. What is being implied is that if Music is honored, verbal correctness and valid perception will be taken care of likewise. And poetry has been much about this last statement. Music in poetry is a way of being just to reality as unseen and reality as having clear impact. Within Verlaine's poem—I'm not forgetting demurs at some phrases—is one of the great presentations of poetic purpose. Reality, made something else than that finally seized by a self or clenched by it, is reality more usefully apprehended, more healthfully respected.

112. *The Idea of Beauty Is Adored in This World, By Joachim du Bellay*. 1967. More than one thing can be said about beauty or poetry

which is true. In Verlaine's *Art Poétique,* poetry (or beauty) is a possibility hovering about or trembling within many, many situations mind can come upon. Poetry trembles in a color of a Parisian morning at 7 A.M., or in a mist over a small French river in the provinces, or in what is beyond a luxurious curtain of a city evening. Poetry then is existence as significantly tremulous. And reality is undoubtedly in motion, is widening, thinning, rising, falling, lighting, darkening, clearer, less clear. But reality is what it is. In the sixteenth century, with the Pléiade, poetry or beauty was given essentially universal firmness, infinite, substantial foundation. In the present poem of Joachim du Bellay, the Verlaine notion of poetry is given a necessary supplement, earlier in time. Du Bellay does not dispute Verlaine, he says more can be said than the tidings of French symbolism. Du Bellay saw beauty as that which was, if nothing else was. Verlaine saw it because everything else was, and beauty mischievously, delicately, subtly, mysteriously, coyly was about, waiting for poetic apprehension musically to give it surprising, undoubted but suggestive, being. This sonnet, then, is the Renaissance or Platonic questioning prelude to Verlaine's sliding deification of the vague. The aesthetic deity of Du Bellay first exists in untroubled abstraction, undisturbed universality. Later he may go about, chat with, become friendly with that grand thing—likely God—which Verlaine calls *l'Indécis.* Verlaine does speak of where the Wavering and the Precise join. And it isn't only in a *chanson grise.* Where the Wavering and the Precise join is where Verlaine and Du Bellay will see that beauty, poetry, reality were thought of well by both.

113. *Ecstasy, By Victor Hugo.* 1967. One can feel, in looking at Victor Hugo's *Extase* of *Les Orientales* of 1829, that the Lord God or *le Seigneur Dieu* the poet sees is like the eternal beauty of Du Bellay and the *musique avant tout chose* of Verlaine. In the *Ecstasy* of Hugo, the writer asks what the source was of "the waters of the sea, the fires of the sky." The composed stars, ever so many, and the unified waves, ever so many, say it is God only that or who could present so much with so much order. Besides order, there is strangeness; and only the Lord God as artist could make that the strangeness of which could awe a mind of France in the 1820's. Hugo says often that the best time to see God is when one is alone: it is also true that God can be seen while one is in a large assemblage. Hugo sees nothingness, confusion, substance at once. Water, fire, space combine. The combining is so thorough, so just, so large, a cause which can combine is felt. Beauty, poetry, art as themselves can be seen in two ways: one, a rather passive, endless source or repository; two, a combining, creating, insisting force which uses a mind, and which a mind can represent. Here the source of sky and night by the sea of Hugo, the Music of Verlaine, and the Eternally Abstract Beauty of Du Bellay seem quite alike.

113. *Reality Is the Source of the Tedious and, Itself, Is Often Tedious.* 1968. If reality is omnipresent, all possibility, everything, uncharted, in-

finite—then, in a way, everything you can say of it is true. Can a statement be made which is not true about something—if only itself? As soon as anything ugly is contemplated, or as a German philosopher might say, is posited, the thing contemplated, as contemplated, is of reality; and the thing posited is of reality, too. Reality has a measureless capacity of welcoming and assimilating nonsense, the objectionable, the distressing, and the ugly. Without reality, there would be no notion of boredom whatsoever. There is nothing blamable which reality cannot be blamed for. So if it's bad, reality has it. What other things may not have or may keep away from, reality welcomes and shelters. The obviousness of all this is indescribable. There is some association of reality with interest: it is hard to say a thing is real without the person saying this, thinking the thing is interesting. Yet this is a mistake. Reality is all that leaves you cold, too. The poem implies that it is useful to engage in two mental purposes or motions at once: the first is to make the thing as real as possible, and the other to make it as tedious as possible. If, however, by some chance, the tedious, unengaging, tepid, flat—the more one makes it real, the more interesting it becomes, then we can see that if a thing is dull, it is not because it is real or unreal, but because, whatever it is, we haven't made it real enough. The relation of the real to the painful has still to be seen adequately. Is pain an aspect of more reality or of less reality, of full reality or partial reality? However this may be, it is well to see the tedious or tiresome as real as the stirring and enthralling. Then it may be good to go on from there.

114. *You Can't Miss the Absolute.* 1955. Is there something unchanging in everything we look at? Does a match have Being? Does a match have Part and Whole? Does a match have Within and Without? Does a match have Manyness and Oneness? Is the match all change and vanishing or is there something which can be said to be in the match, which was before the match, was while the match was visible, touchable, and will be when the match seems not to be around? Is a thing just *of* Existence? Is a thing just to be found *in* Existence? Is a thing just an instance of Existence, or is Existence in a thing? If Existence was able to be a match years ago, was Existence already in a match? Where is the absolute, if not in what seems to be not absolute? How could the infinite, without the temporary, be whatsoever?—The purport of the present poem is that it is impossible to think of illusion without a background of what is not illusion; and further, it is impossible to think of everything in illusion being only illusion, for illusion must have something in it showing it to be illusion. The disproof of what is said about a thing cannot lie only outside the thing; and since the disproof of the relative is something called the absolute, the absolute must be in the relative. The part of the relative, or in the relative, which is the absolute, is the Is or Isness aspect of the relative. When we say the relative is, the verb *is* is in the relative, and is absolute, for Is cannot be thought of as not being Is. So if the relative is, the being of the relative

itself or the Is aspect is absolute. If the relative is not, then the relative has the absolute of Nothing or Is Not. To say that anything is, is to give the absolute of Is to it; to say that anything is not, is to give the Is Not absolute to it. In the section of the poem marked 2: if something does not correspond to something, then it is by itself or is in itself, that is: it is absolute. If something corresponds to something, what is that which it corresponds to? How big and unchanging is it? And is the thing corresponded to in the corresponding thing? Ontologically, everything that a thing is in, is also in that thing. So, if something is in light, light is in that thing likewise. We say that a thing is in motion when we also mean motion is now in that thing. The absolute is then either absent from ordinary things or it is not absent. If it is absent, then the absolute itself is limited, conditioned, relative. What we'd have is the absolute-relative (the absolute absent from the relative) and the relative-absolute (the relative absent from the absolute). But we have neither of these. We have the absolute present in the relative as a circle is present in a small button; and we have the relative present in the absolute as the same small button is present in that existence which is timeless, infinite, unconditioned as such.—Looking at Section 3: if the absolute is not in a mistake of ours, again this absolute is not everywhere; and that means it is not the absolute, for its existence is accompanied by and limited by a mistake of ours. The absolute is really a form of everyday existence, and is the eternity and the boundless present in every datum, item, and object. The Thing in Itself is that which is constant and repeats itself as itself in everything we see, hear, touch, smell, taste. If the absolute is not in the empirical, it is a second-class absolute, which means it is not absolute. The best thing about the infinite is, it doesn't need the infinite to be in. It carries its own place, and this place can be in any place or thing.

115. Femmes Damnées, *By Charles Baudelaire.* 1963. In the *Femmes Damnées* of Baudelaire, or *Women Damned,* there are two women managing the world through each other. Lesbianism, like other forms of sex, is a means of world conquest through the ownership and manipulation of body. There is a sneer in all such ownership which makes the love impure. It is not body which makes love impure, it is the sneer. And the word *impure,* even as Baudelaire uses it, is related to the absolute. We either use a person to love everythingness, the universe, or the Absolute-in-things; or we are limited, which means there is some inaccurate love of ourselves. When Hippolyta, in the second stanza, seeks the *ciel déjà lointain*—"the sky, already far away"—Baudelaire is showing some awareness of the absolute as a thing gone for in ourselves. Complete purity is the absolute, and no one talks of going after incomplete purity, or "relative" purity. We go after purity, and that's that; we don't go after purity, and that's that.—And Baudelaire is concerned with the absolute again in the twenty-third line of the poem—*Et cette gratitude infinie et sublime.* If Baudelaire had no thought at all of the abstract or absolute's being concerned with the Lesbian situation of the poem, why should he use the word *infinite*

at all; or *sublime?* A further notion of something of the absolute is in the phrase, *les grands lacs transparents*—"large clear lakes"—of the eighth stanza. The absolute and relative are somehow both present in the last line of the ninth stanza: *Toi, mon âme et mon coeur, mon tout et ma moitié*—"You, my soul and my heart, my all, my half of me." And the large world is present in a fashion in the phrase: *tes yeux pleins d'azur et d'étoiles*—"your eyes, full of blue and of stars" (tenth stanza). Either Baudelaire is factitiously uttering grandiose sentiment, or he is having Delphine show an inclination to have the world through Hippolyta. It is not by chance that the words of love, including Lesbian love, have in them some import equivalent to existence itself. When Hippolyta answers Delphine and talks of her ways being closed by *un horizon sanglant*— "a bleeding horizon" (stanza twelve), she also shows that the bodies concerned have a wide geography. Within the geography or landscape in space, is a closedness one can fear; and the closedness is related to ego as narrowing. Hippolyta is uncertain, but she feels that while infinity, the absolute—*un rêve sans fin*—"a dream without end" (tenth stanza)— seems to be gone after, the diminution of self results. Hippolyta is afraid the largeness of self will be used only to possess. She says (stanza nineteen): "I feel enlarging in my being/ A deepening abyss; this abyss is my heart." It cannot be said that Baudelaire concludes the poem with summarizing clearness: hardly. The purpose at the moment is to show that Baudelaire was impelled to include the infinite, the absolute, the universe, purity in a poem telling of Lesbians of Paris in the 1850's or so. Baudelaire in the last stanza condemns the way of these Lesbians as sharply as a Monsignor might. Even as he condemns, Baudelaire includes the infinite. The last line of the poem reads: *Et fuyez l'infini que vous portez en vous!*—"And flee the infinite you have within you." The Baudelairean malediction likewise welcomes a synonym of the absolute.

118. *The Oak and the Reed, By Jean de La Fontaine.* 1966. Cajolery and force have been two constant ways men have had of getting their point, or making their point successfully. We yield to win and we fight to win. There are strategy and bopping as means to victory. Force and persuasiveness are related to the makeup of the world as matter and something else. The oak in the La Fontaine fable does not know everything about power; and it is possible the reed doesn't either. How resistance and yielding can both be forms of power has not been described yet. This—resistance and yielding as both power—arises from the fact that pride and humility are both strength. Resistance and yielding, pride and humility (or their likes) can work for evil or good. There is a slight implication in the fable that the reed is good and the oak evil—but it doesn't have to be this way. If we look at the word *acquiescent,* we don't know what to feel. There may be a large-hearted, kind person concerned; or there may be a supple knave, or a resilient sharpy. The word *affable* also has two faces. The answer to all this lies in the structure of the La

Fontaine fable, when it is doing well. The fable, being poetry, has the firmness of the oak and the bendingness of the reed. And now it is about time, while praising this fable, to write another.

119. *Slanting Soft White on Mountain Is Never Through.* 1968. White is the philosophic color, but it is also of the material world, squarely. The white sheep on a mountain weighed as much as if it were black. Another kind of white is in the cloud, which, also, as rain could be tangible, heard, finally earthy. Cloud, mountain, sheep leisurely present a universe teasingly both immaterial and weighty. Loneliness is of abstract white, of physical white, of diagonal once in Asia. The sheep, while diagonal on a mountain, can say something to aspects of machinery, energetic possibilities of physics. We can be like the space around the mountain, the cloud, the sheep, the white. These can meet pistons, teeth, pounding, table; so can we. The world not so well seen, or unseen, and the unquestionably visual world have many ways of hovering about each other. A concealed dance of material and immaterial, of darkness and white, is meant in the poem.

120. *Local Stop, Sheridan Square.* 1966. There are places in America known because something happened there and people wanted to remember what happened. Something happened near Concord Bridge—and it was remembered, among others by Emerson in a poem; something happened at Little Round Top in the neighborhood of Gettysburg, and that too is remembered. Then there are places where something goes on or occurs, and there is no one great occurrence cherished by an historian or poet. The place written of in this poem is where there was Expectation and there was Strangeness and there was the New-and-the-Old as one thing: for there was the "heard of" now become the visible. When people emerged from the subway stop at Sheridan Square, they did feel a little like Columbus on a new shore, or like a New Englander at last in the town of England associated with his dear genealogy. Surely, there are differences; yet there is no doubt that Sheridan Square—the seeing of it —has caused emotion. The emotion was different in 1916, in 1926, in 1936, in 1946, in 1956, and in 1966—but an emotion was. With all the prevalence of the Greenwich Village Weltanschauung and Selbstanschauung —less picturesquely, Worldview and Selfview—in many parts of the country other than Greenwich Village, this portion of New York is irreplaceable in the redolent, thoughtful, sinister, unrestrained possibilities of feminine and masculine America. Something of why, it is hoped, is in the poem. The Long Island shore could be written of in lines of many syllables by that Long Islander, Brooklyner, Manhattaner, and Greenwich Villager, Walt Whitman. Sheridan Square, Local Stop, deserves some long lines too, the melody of which has been thought about.

122. *Hell, Questions, Answers.* 1961. There is the hell of insufficient life. The central thing in life is our questions and answers, and the manner of our having and getting these. If we are not interested in some questions, life is mild, not having its full effect. And if a possible answer does not move us, we also are citizens of the tepid and burghers of torpor. The fact that knowledge is in the world is an indication that the world can be asked about, maybe even wants to be asked about. A person is uneducated, the intensity and force of whose impersonal questions are too below the intensity and force with which he has questions about his own life, only that. The world was made a world, or is a world, to stir one into the desire to know and the desire to organize and make powerful what one knows. Consequently, if the questions we might have are not asked or are asked often but with an absence of adequate interest, are asked by a mildly fluttering unconscious, a kind of hell is present: the hell in which life goes on, but life doesn't wholly welcome or admire life. In man, life does look at life and has an opinion of it. If, then, life asks questions, but dully and half-heartedly, the answers will not be satisfactory, will not be lively. The absence of life through something narrow, exclusive, ego-given in a living being, is the presence, as was said, of some kind of hell in that living being. Certain cantos of Dante's *Inferno* accord well with the notion of the infernal being self-chosen diminution of life by a person. If we, through conceit, make our lives less, we are requesting hell and, likely, getting it. At this time, our questions are incomplete, and the answers we get are not whole. The being doomed by our choice to a lesser, curtailed, flatter and more fearful existence, is what the idea of hell begins with. The change from tepidity to pain was a useful attempt to dramatize tepidity. The fear that often is along with chosen tepidity for one's life and as one's life, could make hell a place of pain. Our notion, though, is that hell was asked for when ego made the world less, and less engaging than it is; and fear, which was the beginning of pain, came to self at this time. All the while, questions and answers were not as stirring as they could be.

122. *Our Leader.* 1965. Our times will be seen some day as times in which absence of feeling coldly and slickly prevailed. Man has found it expedient, in his effort to protect himself and to establish himself, to feel selectively, which usually means insufficiently. Flagrant in absence of feeling, distinguished in narrowness of emotion, representative in coldness about what does not immediately concern him or which can not add to the success of vanity—there is America's Chief Executive. The manner in which Chief Executive Johnson kept away from the pain of distant beings and the ethical questioning of many persons in America is a tremendous achievement in emotional segregation, in frigidity of heart. Our Chief Executive has made calm in itself a virtue or quality, not seeing that calm, when ethics is deeply and movingly concerned, is a defect. All religions have seen absence of feeling as an insult to the Lord

or the Divine. It is what we are calm about, not just our being calm, that makes us just or strong. Our Chief Executive never said a word regretting the use of napalm, let alone a word asking for or hoping for its not being used. It seems he thought, and many others with power and possessions also did, that by not recognizing the use by the American military forces of this cruelly terrifying and terrifyingly cruel means of killing and disabling human beings, our Chief Executive was mindful of the national interest. What is said in the poem is quite true. Our Chief Executive, because he was calm, or appeared calm when others had seen horror—for this our Chief Executive asked national approval. He has not got it entirely. Long live humanity! Long live America!

122. *Boredom Hard to Perceive in Prehistory*. 1961. Prehistory, though having flint, stone, water, caves, fire, and living beings, chiefly human, consists of so much blankness, vagueness, lack of incident. Prehistory lacks the particular, and is that much like space as such, or infinity, which likewise lacks the particular. Prehistoric man knew so much, for after all he was chiefly man. However, he also did not know so much. The way we are like prehistoric man is in what we don't know. Ignorance, like infinity or space, lacks lively particularity and the organization of lively particularity with other lively particularity. Prehistoric man appears to be so much in a state of active dream, food-getting, fire-making, woman-having, he wasn't in a position, as far as life went, to be bored. Boredom occurs when you know something of great, sharp interest and can't have this great, sharp interest. The causes of boredom are exclusiveness as emptiness in oneself; and the fact that the world can be seen as flat, continuous and dull aloofness; something which is, but doesn't ask successfully to be known. Boredom is a conspiracy of the possessive, not-seeing self and a world which can seem external and aloof. This much of prehistory is ours. The world as something completing ourselves and therefore to be known, is not that sufficiently for us. The purpose of poetry is to make the world our own, while not possessing it in any ugly manner at all. We have left prehistory, but we have not got fully to history—the seeing of what the world was and is as something which is ourselves. Hail, (possible) American Development!

INDEX OF TITLES

191

INDEX OF TRANSLATIONS